A TACTICAL WORK BOOK AND LIFE GUIDE

THE
ABORTED
MALE

REVERSING THE TACTICS AND SCHEMES OF
THE MODERN DAY PHARAOHS

Y. S. SALEEM

CONTENTS

INTRODUCTION

In a world of shifting roles and expectations, the concept of manhood eludes him. He finds himself caught in a tangled web of contradictions, not knowing where to turn. Believing that he can fake it until he makes it, he dons a mask of confidence, unaware that he is still a counterfeit version of himself. His days are consumed by emotional and mental self-indulgence, a futile attempt to find solace in the midst of his confusion.

Work becomes secondary to pleasure and play, as his misinformed peers convince him that crime and violence are more lucrative and fitting for the modern identity. His passion and desires become his guiding principles, leading him down a treacherous path. He adopts the motto, "If loving crime and violence is wrong, then I don't want to do right."

Learning becomes an afterthought, as he convinces himself that the streets hold all the wisdom he needs. Lifelong learning becomes an alien concept, and his mind remains closed to the possibilities that education and personal growth can offer. He slowly becomes socially isolated and obsolete, without realizing the depth of his regression.

Responsibility terrifies him, as the fear of failure consumes his thoughts. His ego shields him from accepting the weight of responsibility, and he finds himself deflecting blame onto others. Rational lies, self-deception, and denial become his arsenal, all in a desperate attempt to preserve the illusion of his competence. But deep down, he lives in constant fear of being exposed as a fraud.

Uncertainty and doubt haunt his every step. He interprets every cry or comment as a personal attack, fearing that any sign of weakness or vulnerability will render him powerless. He yearns for things without earning them, convinced that shortcuts exist for those who know better than others. The pursuit of immediate gratification becomes his guiding principle, blinding him to the value of hard work and perseverance.

Education and personal experience hold no weight in his eyes. He rejects any attempt to impart knowledge, dismissing it as irrelevant noise. He turns to popular media, dopamine hits, and the toxic allure of street life as his university, unaware of the shallowness of his understanding.

Money and credit become constant sources of struggle. His lack of financial discipline leads him to squander resources and seek refuge in the generosity of others. Saving becomes an abstract concept, overshadowed by impulsive decisions driven by compulsive habits. He finds himself caught in a cycle of instant gratification, unable to break free.

Women enter his life with the hope of transforming him into a man, but their efforts are in vain. He is lost in his own confusion, unable to cultivate a sense of self or establish meaningful relationships. His values are rooted in materialism, fixated on tangible possessions rather than embracing the depths of spirituality. Vulnerability is a foreign concept, as he obsessively guards his image, willing to go to extreme lengths to fit in and gain the approval of his peers.

In the distorted realm of his perception, he believes that women cannot exist without him. He sees himself as the center of the universe, a legend in his own mind. He lacks the understanding of how to cultivate himself or navigate relationships with women. Leadership eludes him, as he struggles to find his true identity.

He is consumed by self-absorption, trapped in a cycle of narcissism. Frustration becomes a breeding ground for cruelty and sociopathic tendencies. When he feels hurt, he inflicts pain upon others, using language or emotional manipulation as weapons. Domestic violence becomes a twisted means of asserting control when things don't go his way.

Co-dependency entangles many of his relationships, as he lacks a solid sense of self. Recognition by the group becomes his sole purpose, overshadowing any semblance of true identity. In the mirror, he is faced with self-hate, projected onto those who resemble him. Subconsciously dissatisfied with himself, he harbors an eagerness to punish the world for his own shortcomings.

In the depths of his journey, he seeks to unmask the challenges of masculinity and embark on a path of personal growth.

This is the story of the Aborted Male, a narrative that confronts the complexities and struggles of modern manhood. It is a journey towards self-discovery, a call to break free from the chains that bind him, and a search for authentic masculinity and a life of fulfillment.

CHAPTER ONE

————◆◆◊◆◆————

THE ABORTED MALE IS NOT A NATURAL CULTURAL PROGRESSION, BUT A PLAN TO CONTROL AND MANIPULATE FOR GAIN

In the journey of self-discovery and personal growth, one essential aspect that the Aborted Male must confront is the challenge of personal responsibility and discipline. This chapter explores the themes of self-accountability, the importance of discipline, and strategies for cultivating these qualities in order to overcome the obstacles that hinder growth and success.

The Aborted Male often struggles with taking responsibility for his actions and the outcomes of his choices. Blaming others for personal failures becomes a common defense mechanism, shielding him from facing the truth about his own contributions to the situation. This unwillingness to accept responsibility keeps him trapped in a cycle of stagnation, preventing him from experiencing true growth and self-improvement.

To break free from this pattern, the Aborted Male must first recognize the power and freedom that comes with embracing personal responsibility. It is not an admission of fault or weakness, but rather a courageous acknowledgment that he has the ability to influence his own life and create the future he desires. Taking ownership of his choices empowers him to make conscious decisions, learn from mistakes, and actively shape his destiny. Look, no one is going to be more involved in your life than you! So no matter the help received, you're the cultivator of your soul.

However, accepting personal responsibility alone is not enough. It must be accompanied by the cultivation of discipline—another trait often lacking in the Aborted Male's life. Without discipline, his thinking becomes scattered, his actions inconsistent, and his progress hindered. He may be easily swayed by external influences or fall prey to the allure of short-term pleasures, prioritizing immediate gratification over long-term growth. In other words a maladaptive response to a problem becomes the answer, the practice and habit until it flourishes as the preferred lifestyle. This lifestyle eventually corrupts the character, and in turn the subconscious mind becomes the beast from within.

Developing discipline requires a commitment to self-mastery and self-control. It involves setting clear goals, creating routines and systems, and staying focused on the desired outcomes. By establishing healthy habits and sticking to them, the Aborted Male can gradually build discipline in various areas of his life. This may include implementing structured daily routines, practicing time-management techniques, and setting achievable targets.

In addition to discipline, the Aborted Male must also cultivate self-awareness. This involves developing an understanding of his strengths, weaknesses, triggers, and patterns of behavior. Through introspection and reflection, he can identify areas for improvement and implement strategies to overcome challenges. Mindfulness practices, such as meditation and journaling, can be valuable tools for developing self-awareness and gaining insights into one's thoughts and emotions.

Furthermore, seeking support and guidance from mentors, coaches, or support groups can provide accountability and guidance on the path of personal growth. Engaging in meaningful conversations and learning from those who have walked a similar journey can offer valuable perspectives and insights. He needs to seek out men who ignore comfort yet insist on self-cultivation. Men who walk the earth with a relaxed certainty, who seem to respect all life, and seem to flourish and enjoy casual contact with all people—but especially women, without any sense of exploitation or harassment.

In the pursuit of personal growth and masculinity, the Aborted Male must grapple with the delicate balance between pleasure and responsibility. This chapter delves into the challenges of finding equilibrium, the impact of cultural influences on decision-making, and strategies for cultivating emotional intelligence, self-regulation skills, and restorative practices.

In a society driven by instant gratification and pleasure-seeking, the Aborted Male often finds himself drawn more towards immediate pleasures and indulgences rather than shouldering responsibilities. This imbalance can hinder his personal growth and render him ineffective in his pursuit of authenticity and fulfillment. This imbalance is easily seen by women, whose nature seeks security and strength for the possibility of new life coming through them. Women need men of strength and purpose, not pleasure-seeking hollow male manikins making excuses for only having an image of a man, but not the content of character. Women know, "The chatter don't matter." Milk, housing, and diapers are never paid with an excuse. As the popular saying among women goes, "I can do bad by myself."

However, to be fair, there are sciences and systems used by cultural influencers to create these sociopathic syndromes in the modern male that are very difficult to ignore or escape. To understand this dynamic, we must explore the concept of agnotology—the study of culturally induced ignorance. Agnotology examines the schemes and subliminal strategies used by cultural influencers to reduce awareness of the consequences of pursuing pleasure and avoiding discomfort. The Aborted Male may be subtly influenced by societal norms and messages that prioritize pleasure over responsibility, leading to a diminished awareness of the long-term impact of his actions. These sciences are easy to understand once they are examined separately. However, these behavioral and cognitive schemes systematically use formulas that include, chemistry, biology, marketing, social science, sensory information, and math to create a consensus trance that works primarily on the subconscious level, so they're not easily noticed.

Breaking Free from the Modern-Day Pharaohs

In ancient times, the scriptural metaphor of a Pharaoh depicted a ruler who intentionally slaughtered men, enslaved women and children, and sought to exert complete dominance over the people of Egypt. Fast forward to the present day, and we find that similar schemes and strategies are being employed by the modern-day Pharaohs to limit the opportunities for boys to become responsible men. These tactics systematically remove leadership from the mind of the male, his family system, his neighborhood, his community, and eventually, the entire nation. The result is the robbing of generations of men who could have cultivated strength, purpose, and integrity, instead leaving behind a trail of soul-less predators and contributing to the toxic culture we witness today.

The Aborted Male, caught in the web of these insidious techniques, often remains oblivious to the deliberate tactics employed to diminish his sense of masculinity and manhood. He is left unaware of the forces that undermine his potential and thwart his growth. As noted by reference to subliminal conditioning in the introduction, there is a profound truth that resonates with another expression:

"If you can control a man's thinking, you do not have to worry about his actions. When you determine what a man shall think, you do not have to concern yourself about what he will do. If you make a man feel that he is inferior, you do not have to compel him to accept an inferior status, for he will seek it himself. If you make a man think that he is justly an outcast, you do not have to order him to the back door. He will go without being told, and if there is no back door, his very nature will demand one."

– Carter G. Woodson

With this understanding, it becomes crucial to embark on a journey of self-discovery and reclaiming one's identity as a man. It is time to break free from the clutches of the modern-day Pharaohs and their manipulative tactics. This book serves as a guide, shining a light on the hidden strategies that have diminished masculinity and deprived men of their rightful place in society. It offers insights, skills, and actionable steps to counteract negative influences and restore a sense of purpose, strength, and authenticity.

The road to liberation requires a holistic approach, addressing physical, spiritual, emotional, and intellectual growth. It necessitates a deep examination of the self, a willingness to confront the wounds and insecurities that have been imposed upon the aborted male. Through self-regulation skills, emotional intelligence, mindfulness practices, and the cultivation of diplomatic and Zen-like attitudes, it is possible to break free from the chains of false narratives and reclaim one's power.

This book is a call to action for men who find themselves troubled by the stereotypical roles they have been assigned and the limitations they face. This book is also a helpful reference for the many daughters, girlfriends, sisters, wives and mothers who love these males; but need them to be wise, emotionally balanced, spiritual

14

grounded and cultivated as men of strength and responsibility in their lives. It is a call to reject the toxic norms and embrace a path of personal transformation and societal change. By embracing self-love, self-acceptance, and a deep understanding of one's own unique value, men can step into their true potential as leaders, cultivators, builders and characters that are universally admired and respected.

Let us embark on this journey together, armed with the knowledge, skills, and motivation to overcome the influence of the modern-day Pharaohs. It is time to break free from the chains that bind us, rewrite our own narratives, and create a new paradigm of masculinity. The power lies within us, waiting to be reclaimed. Always seize the opportunity when it presents itself.

To overcome these challenges, several readily available skills can help and assist the Aborted Male with self-cultivation. One of several needed skills is Emotional Intelligence (EQ) to navigate the complexities of pleasure and responsibility. EQ encompasses self-awareness, self-regulation, empathy, and interpersonal skills, all of which contribute to effective decision-making and personal growth.

1. **Self-Awareness:** Developing self-awareness allows the Aborted Male to recognize his tendencies towards seeking immediate pleasure and avoiding responsibility. By understanding his emotional triggers, beliefs, and patterns of behavior, he can make conscious choices that align with his long-term goals.

2. **Self-Regulation:** Self-regulation skills are essential for managing impulses, delaying gratification, and staying committed to responsibilities. The Aborted Male can cultivate self-regulation through practices such as mindfulness meditation, deep-breathing exercises, and journaling. These techniques help him develop the capacity to pause, reflect, and make deliberate choices rather than succumbing to impulsive desires.

3. **Empathy:** Empathy allows the Aborted Male to understand the perspectives and feelings of others, fostering healthier relationships and better decision-making. By placing himself in the shoes of those affected by his actions, he can make choices that prioritize the well-being of others alongside his own.

4. **Interpersonal Skills:** Effective communication, active listening, and conflict resolution skills are vital for navigating relationships and taking responsibility for his actions. The Aborted Male can develop these skills through practice, seeking feedback, and engaging in empathetic conversations.

Alongside developing emotional intelligence, the Aborted Male can employ restorative strategies to maintain balance and harmony in his life. Restorative practices involve intentionally engaging in activities that promote well-being, self-reflection, and rejuvenation. These may include hobbies, physical exercise, spending time in nature, practicing gratitude, or engaging in therapy or counseling.

By integrating emotional intelligence, self-regulation skills, and restorative practices into his life, the Aborted Male can find the delicate balance between pleasure and responsibility. He can make conscious choices that honor his long-term goals, while also indulging in healthy pleasures and enjoying life's offerings. This equilibrium empowers him to grow as an authentic, responsible, and fulfilled individual.

The aborted male needs to understand what some of the historical tactics used by every pharaoh are:

Conquerors have historically employed various strategies to make the conquered people willing slaves, often aimed at undermining their sense of identity, independence, and resistance. Although the specific methods may vary, the overall objective is to exert control and ensure compliance. Here are some common strategies employed by conquerors:

1. **Cultural Suppression:** Conquerors may impose their own culture and beliefs on the conquered people, suppressing or eradicating local traditions, languages, and customs. By erasing the cultural identity of the conquered, the conquerors aim to replace it with their own, creating a sense of dependency and subservience.

2. **Divide and Conquer:** Conquerors may exploit existing divisions within the conquered society, such as ethnic or religious differences, to pit different groups against each other. By sowing discord and fostering internal conflicts, they weaken collective

resistance and create a sense of instability that necessitates their continued presence as a controlling force.

3. **Economic Exploitation:** Conquerors often exploit the economic resources of the conquered land, extracting wealth and resources for their own benefit. They may establish systems of taxation, forced labor, or economic monopolies that leave the conquered people impoverished and dependent on the conquerors for sustenance.

4. **Propaganda and Ideological Manipulation:** Conquerors use propaganda and ideological manipulation to shape the narrative and perception of the conquered people. They promote the conquerors' superiority and the inherent inferiority of the conquered, instilling a sense of subservience and justifying their rule. This manipulation of beliefs and ideologies helps in maintaining control and fostering a willingness to serve.

5. **Physical and Psychological Control:** Conquerors may use physical force, oppression, and intimidation to establish control over the conquered population. This includes practices such as enslavement, torture, and punishment, which instill fear and suppress any notions of resistance or rebellion. Through the systematic use of violence and coercion, conquerors maintain their dominance and ensure compliance.

CHAPTER TWO

————◆◆◇◆◆————

CONFRONTING CULTURALLY IMPOSED SHAME AND EMBRACING AUTHENTICITY

In the realm of emotions, shame stands as a formidable presence, often referred to as the vampire of our inner world—a force that drains the life out of individuals. It comes with physical discomfort, dissonance, and psychic hurt that makes it an emotion most try to avoid at all costs. But to truly understand shame and its impact on our lives, we must delve deeper into its nature and explore the transformative journey of confronting shame and embracing authenticity, especially as it relates to the Aborted Male.

Shame arises when we break an agreement that we have made with ourselves, when we stray outside the boundaries of our own internal rules. It acts as a resounding reminder, a faithful voice, which alerts us when we have veered off the path aligned with our values and core beliefs. In some instances, shame can even precede our actions, acting as a preventive force, dissuading us from engaging in behavior that would be incongruent with our authentic selves. Shame is one of the tactics used by the modern-day Pharaoh to keep dissonance in place, as the mind is distracted with noise, conflicting values, constant change and manipulation of cultural norms. In some circles, they applaud all diversity; for some, these new choices in diversity offer the consequence of most things being accepted as normal, preventing a foundation of certainty for many. So, for many males in this new generation of diversity, is the wandering of the mind with its struggle with truth, normalcy, and uncertainty, which feels more like a curse than its promised freedoms.

However, the intricate dance between shame and authenticity is not always straightforward. As we navigate the complexities of the world around us, we can sometimes lose touch with our true nature, succumbing to societal pressures, fears, and anxieties. In doing so, we drift away from authenticity and become false versions of ourselves, engaging in actions that conflict with our core personality and beliefs.

People often adopt a fake persona for various reasons, driven by fear, anxiety, and the discomfort of vulnerability. They fear that if others were to know who they truly are, they would no longer be liked, respected, or even loved. This fear compels them to wear masks and present false versions of themselves, day in and day out.

However, embracing authenticity is a crucial aspect of building healthy, impactful, and meaningful relationships. Genuine connections can only be formed when we allow ourselves to be seen and accepted for who we truly are. Moreover, wearing a constant mask and maintaining a persona can be exhausting. The weight of this facade takes its toll on our energy, leaving us drained and disconnected from our authentic selves. Letting go of the false self and embracing our true nature offers a lighter and more fulfilling way of being.

To confront shame and embark on the journey of authenticity, it is crucial to recognize that shame is not a reflection of our inherent worth or value as individuals. It is a product of societal expectations, internalized beliefs, and past experiences. By understanding the origins of shame and challenging its validity, we can begin to dismantle its power over us.

One essential aspect of this journey is the embrace of sincerity as a lifestyle. Sincerity involves living in alignment with our true selves, free from pretense or masks. It means embracing our imperfections, acknowledging our mistakes, and taking responsibility for our actions. By cultivating sincerity, we create an atmosphere of authenticity in which we can deeply connect with ourselves and others.

While the path to embracing authenticity and shedding shame is unique for everyone, there are practices and self-help skills that can support this transformative process.

1. **Mindfulness:** Mindfulness is the practice of cultivating present-moment awareness without judgment. By developing mindfulness, we become more attuned to our thoughts, emotions, and bodily sensations. This heightened self-awareness allows us to recognize and investigate feelings of shame as

they arise. Through mindfulness, we can observe shame with curiosity and compassion, allowing it to dissipate rather than overpowering us.

Self-Help Exercise: Take a few moments each day to sit in silence and focus on your breath. Allow your thoughts and emotions to arise without judgment or resistance. Notice any feelings of shame that may surface and observe them with gentle curiosity. Remind yourself that these feelings are temporary and do not define your worth.

2. **Faith and Self-Acceptance:** Faith, whether in a higher power, oneself, or the inherent goodness of humanity, can provide a foundation for self-acceptance and the release of shame. Faith allows us to trust in the process of personal growth and to believe in our capacity for change and transformation. By cultivating faith and self-acceptance, we can let go of shame and embrace our authentic selves.

Self-Help Exercise: Engage in practices that nurture your faith, such as prayer, meditation, or connecting with a supportive community. Reflect on moments in your life when you have overcome challenges or experienced personal growth. Use these reflections as reminders of your resilience and capacity for change.

3. **Holistic Diet:** Our physical well-being is intricately linked to our emotional and mental well-being. A holistic diet, rich in nourishing foods, can support

the release of shame and promote overall well-being. Focus on incorporating whole, unprocessed foods, fresh fruits and vegetables, lean proteins, and healthy fats into your meals. Avoid excessive consumption of sugar, caffeine, and processed foods, as they can negatively impact mood and contribute to feelings of shame.

Self-Help Exercise: Take time to plan and prepare nutritious meals for yourself. Experiment with new recipes that incorporate wholesome ingredients. Pay attention to how your body feels when nourished with healthy foods, and notice any positive shifts in your emotional well-being.

4. **Physical Exercise:** Engaging in regular physical exercise is not only beneficial for our physical health but also plays a significant role in improving our mental and emotional well-being. Exercise releases dopamine, endorphins, reduces stress, and promotes a sense of empowerment and self-confidence. By engaging in physical activity, we can strengthen our connection to our bodies and cultivate a positive relationship with ourselves.

Self-Help Exercise: Find a form of exercise that you enjoy, whether it's walking, jogging, dancing, yoga, or any other activity that gets your body moving. Set aside dedicated time each week to engage in this exercise and notice the positive impact it has on your mood and overall sense of well-being.

In summary, confronting shame and embracing authenticity is a transformative journey that requires self-reflection, self-compassion, and a commitment to personal growth. By practicing mindfulness, nurturing faith and self-acceptance, adopting a holistic diet, and engaging in physical exercise, we can release the grip of shame and cultivate a life rooted in authenticity, self-love, and personal fulfillment. Through these self-help skills and exercises, the Aborted Male can embark on a path of healing, growth, and the reclamation of their true identity.

More Hidden Power of Shame

To be truly authentic, and feel a worthy identity, one must strive for transparency in their thoughts, actions, and relationships. Transparency requires a willingness to be open, honest, and vulnerable. However, achieving transparency can be hindered by the presence of shame. Shame acts as a barrier, causing individuals to hide aspects of themselves that they perceive as flawed or unworthy.

Keeping secrets demands a tremendous amount of energy from our nervous system. Constantly being on alert, carefully choosing our words, monitoring the reactions of others, and searching for any clues that our secret may be exposed requires a high level of mental and physical effort. This hypervigilance takes a toll on our immune system, our ability to communicate, and our relationships. Those burdened by shame may find themselves withdrawing from relationships and communication, fearing the exposure of their secret. This avoidance and the resulting stress can lead to delusion, isolation, aggression, and other maladaptive behaviors.

Over time, unresolved shame can evolve into depression, panic attacks, suicidal ideation, and other harmful psychological states. Individuals may seek escape through the use of drugs or other self-destructive behaviors. Shame can create a vicious cycle that perpetuates negative emotions, thoughts, and actions, ultimately diminishing our overall well-being.

Embracing Sincerity

Embracing sincerity as a lifestyle becomes crucial in this process. Sincerity involves living in alignment with one's true self, devoid of pretense or masks, and not being afraid to be present. It means embracing imperfections, acknowledging mistakes, and holding on to a quiet mind and spirit as you observe the energy, impact, or intensity of these feelings and emotions and taking responsibility for their creation and consequences without falling apart or blaming others. Sincerity creates an atmosphere of authenticity, a path back to the constellation of one's humanity where individuals can reconnect deeply with themselves and others.

To cultivate sincerity, individuals must practice self-reflection and introspection. They must be willing to confront their fears, insecurities, and past traumas. This may involve seeking therapy, engaging in healing practices, and surrounding themselves with a supportive community. By doing so, they can begin to unravel the layers of shame, unveiling their true selves with compassion and self-acceptance.

Living without shame and embracing sincerity requires courage and resilience. It means stepping into the discomfort of vulnerability, risking judgment and rejection. However, the rewards are immense. By letting go of shame and embracing sincerity, individuals can experience profound personal growth, deep connections, and a profound sense of inner peace.

There is an inherent truth that no one can be more involved in your life than you. It emphasizes the importance of taking personal responsibility for one's own actions, choices, and overall well-being.

At the core of this statement lies the understanding that you are the primary driver of your own life. While external factors and influences undoubtedly shape our experiences, it is ultimately up to each individual to navigate their own journey and make decisions that align with their values, goals, and aspirations.

Taking ownership of your life means recognizing that you have agency and control over your thoughts, actions, and attitudes. It means understanding that you have the power to shape your own destiny and create the life you desire. This mindset empowers you to make proactive choices, overcome challenges, and pursue personal growth and fulfillment.

Being involved in your own life requires self-awareness and introspection. It means taking the time to reflect on your values, passions, and purpose. By understanding yourself on a deeper level, you can make more informed decisions that align with your authentic self and lead to greater satisfaction and fulfillment.

Additionally, being actively involved in your life necessitates taking responsibility for your actions and their consequences. It means acknowledging and learning from your mistakes, as well as celebrating your successes. It requires a willingness to embrace challenges, step out of your comfort zone, and take calculated risks in pursuit of personal growth and meaningful experiences.

While external support, guidance, and connections with others are valuable, ultimately you are the one who must take the initiative to create the life you envision. You have the power to set goals, make plans, and take action towards achieving them. This self-directed approach to life enables you to cultivate resilience, adaptability, and a sense of purpose.

Recognizing that no one is going to be more involved in your life than yourself is a powerful realization. It highlights the importance of taking personal responsibility, being self-aware, and actively pursuing personal growth and fulfillment. There is no authenticity without you being present and involved in your own life, more than anyone else.

In the upcoming chapters, we will delve deeper into the practices and skills necessary to cultivate transparency, eliminate shame, and embrace sincerity as a lifestyle.

Through practical strategies, introspective exercises, and real-life examples, the Aborted Male will discover the power of living authentically and the transformative impact it can have on personal growth and relationships.

CHAPTER THREE

————◆◆◊◆◆————

EMBRACING LIFELONG LEARNING FOR PERSONAL GROWTH AND CULTURAL ADAPTATION

In a rapidly evolving world characterized by technological advancements and shifting cultural norms, the Aborted Male faces the critical challenge of remaining current and avoiding obsolescence. This chapter explores the significance of lifelong learning as a means to cultivate strong intelligence, qualify for family and community leadership, and become a transformative force in an increasingly toxic and morally weakened cultural environment.

To thrive in today's complex and dynamic society, the Aborted Male must recognize the importance of continuous learning. Lifelong learning goes beyond formal education and encompasses a mindset of curiosity, adaptability, and a commitment to personal growth. It is an ongoing process that allows individuals to acquire new knowledge, skills, and perspectives throughout their lives, ensuring that they remain relevant and agile in the face of ever-changing circumstances.

One of the key benefits of embracing lifelong learning is the cultivation of strong intelligence. As new technologies emerge and information becomes more readily accessible, individuals who engage in continuous learning can broaden their intellectual horizons and stay abreast of current trends and developments. By actively seeking out new knowledge and challenging their existing beliefs, the Aborted Male can expand his understanding of the world and develop critical thinking skills that enable him to navigate complex issues with clarity and depth.

Moreover, lifelong learning serves as a qualifier for family and community leadership. In an era marked by uncertainty and rapid change, leadership requires individuals who possess a broad knowledge base, an ability to adapt, and a commitment to serving others. By consistently acquiring new skills and insights, the Aborted Male positions himself as a reliable and respected figure within his family and community. He becomes someone whom others turn to for guidance, support, and innovative solutions to the challenges they face.

Lifelong learning also equips the Aborted Male to remain transformative in the face of a toxic and morally weakened cultural environment. The modern world presents numerous challenges, such as increasing polarization, diminishing ethical standards, and an erosion of moral character. By engaging in ongoing learning, the Aborted Male can develop a strong moral compass and cultivate the values necessary to counteract these negative influences. He becomes a beacon of integrity, compassion, and wisdom, capable of effecting positive change in his immediate surroundings and beyond.

To actively embrace lifelong learning, the Aborted Male can adopt several practices and strategies:

1. **Curiosity:** Cultivating a sense of curiosity allows the Aborted Male to maintain an open mind and a hunger for knowledge. By embracing new experiences, exploring diverse perspectives, and asking thought-provoking questions, he continuously expands his intellectual and emotional horizons.

2. **Self-Reflection:** Regular self-reflection enables the Aborted Male to assess his strengths, weaknesses, and areas for improvement. Through introspection, he can identify his passions, interests, and areas of expertise, guiding his learning journey towards areas that align with his values and aspirations.

3. **Learning Communities:** Engaging with learning communities, whether through online platforms, local groups, or mentorship programs, provides opportunities for collaboration, sharing of ideas, and mutual support. Interacting with like-minded individuals fosters a culture of learning and encourages the exchange of diverse perspectives.

4. **Continuous Skill Development:** The Aborted Male should actively seek opportunities to develop and refine his skills. This can include enrolling in relevant courses, attending workshops or seminars, or seeking mentorship from experts in his chosen field.

By honing his skills, he positions himself as a valuable asset and a lifelong learner.

5. **Holistic Growth:** Lifelong learning encompasses not only intellectual pursuits but also emotional, physical, and spiritual development. The Aborted Male should prioritize his well-being by engaging in practices such as mindfulness, physical exercise, and spiritual nourishment. These practices provide the foundation for a balanced and fulfilling life.

Embracing lifelong learning is essential for the Aborted Male's personal growth, cultural adaptation, and leadership qualifications. By remaining current, avoiding obsolescence, cultivating strong intelligence, and fostering transformative qualities, he becomes a force of positive change in an increasingly toxic and morally weakened cultural environment. Through curiosity, self-reflection, engagement with learning communities, continuous skill development, and holistic growth, the Aborted Male can navigate the complexities of the modern world with confidence, resilience, and a commitment to lifelong learning.

Revising the Internal Vocabulary

It is crucial to recognize the power of the internal cultural vocabulary in shaping one's identity and resilience. The Aborted Male must understand that his internal narrative and self-perception should transcend the toxic cultural influences that may have targeted him for mental and emotional destruction in the past.

It is important to acknowledge that many individuals, including the Aborted Male, have experienced adverse circumstances and trauma during their upbringing. These experiences can have a profound impact on one's sense of self-worth, belief systems, and ability to navigate the challenges of life. Therefore, it is crucial not to solely blame oneself for not knowing or for the struggles faced along the journey.

To live as a new man, the Aborted Male must accept his innate power and recognize that he was created to be powerful regardless of his past. This means acknowledging that external cultural influences do not define his worth or potential. He must tap into his internal strength, resilience, and unique qualities to break free from the limitations imposed by societal expectations and negative experiences.

By developing a transcendent internal cultural vocabulary, the Aborted Male can cultivate a mindset of empowerment, self-belief, and self-compassion. This involves reframing negative beliefs and self-talk, replacing them with positive affirmations that reinforce his worth, capabilities, and potential for growth. He must learn to embrace his authentic self, free from the constraints imposed by societal norms or past traumas.

Building a strong internal cultural vocabulary also requires surrounding oneself with supportive and empowering influences. This may involve seeking out positive role models, mentors, or a community of individuals who share similar values and aspirations. These connections can provide encouragement, guidance, and a sense of belonging, reinforcing the Aborted Male's belief in his own power and potential.

Additionally, engaging in healing practices, such as therapy, counseling, or self-reflection exercises, can aid in the process of addressing and healing from past wounds. These practices can help the Aborted Male navigate and transform the internal dialogue, allowing him to release self-blame and embrace a more empowering narrative.

Ultimately, by recognizing the influence of the internal cultural vocabulary, the Aborted Male can transcend the toxic cultural influences that may have impacted his past. Embracing his innate power and worth, he can redefine his identity and embrace a life of personal growth, purpose, and resilience.

Some Disclosure by the Author

On a personal note, I reflected on my own journey in the past as an Aborted Male, as one of the most daunting challenges I faced was nurturing a sense of responsibility while battling the overwhelming fear of failure. It seemed that society's expectations of a man's role had become obscured for me, leaving me uncertain and hesitant to show up fully without excuses. I observed other men avoiding commitments such as marriage and fatherhood, and I couldn't help but wonder if it was because they, too, were burdened by a culture that expected them to fail.

The fear of failure lurked within me, gnawing at my confidence and paralyzing my actions. It whispered insidious doubts, telling me that I am not capable or knowledgeable enough to succeed. It tempted me to hide my uncertainty, afraid that if I let others know, they would discover my vulnerabilities and weaknesses. This fear became a heavy weight that held me back from fully embracing my role as a responsible man.

In a world that often celebrates bravado and masks vulnerability, it was crucial to acknowledge that not knowing enough is a natural part of the learning process. I had to get out of my own way. Instead of allowing the fear to consume me, I needed to confront the cowardliness head-on and reframe it as an opportunity for growth and self-improvement. Embracing the uncertainty and acknowledging my limitations was the first step toward nurturing responsibility. I remember telling G'd on my knees, "I don't know what I'm doing."

To overcome the fear of failure and uncertainty that plagued my mind, I ran to an environment that encouraged openness, learning, and vulnerability. To myself I acknowledged that no one knows everything, and it was okay to seek knowledge and guidance from others, I had to learn to trust again. Rather than pretending to have all the answers, I finally and arduously accepted a mindset of lifelong learning, continuous self-improvement and seeking and accepting spiritual guidance as a lifestyle. I knew I needed to live well or die ugly.

Taking responsibility also meant showing up authentically and without excuses. It required me to confront the fear of being judged or criticized for my vulnerabilities, by understanding that vulnerability is not a weakness but a strength. I finally let go of the need to appear invincible and allowed myself to be seen as human. This authenticity eventually paved the way for meaningful connections, gratefulness, and genuine growth.

I finally recognized that societal expectations were burdensome and created an atmosphere of pressure and self-doubt. I needed to use faith and trust to challenge these expectations and redefine what it means to be a responsible man. I was fearful and uncomfortable often in the beginning of accepting this new mindset. I learned it was not smart to conform to societal norms but rather accepting to see a new logic of living in alignment with my own values and aspirations. By embracing my unique path and taking ownership of my choices, I could redefine success on my own terms.

In nurturing responsibility, I eventually surrounded myself with new friends and a supportive spiritual community of like-minded individuals. I sought out role models who had faced similar challenges and also triumphed over their fears and could provide inspiration and guidance. I learned for the first time how to engage in open and honest conversations with trusted friends and mentors whose insight and wisdom helped to alleviate the weight of uncertainty and foster a sense of camaraderie.

To address the fear of failure and uncertainty head-on, I focused on scriptural scientific metaphors and practical skills and knowledge to better understand the uncertainty and my own response to it. I began a new journey towards self-education, seeking professional development opportunities, and actively engaging in experiences that pushed me outside of my comfort zone. Each step I took toward personal growth and responsibility strengthened my confidence and ability to navigate the challenges that lay ahead.

This short first-person narrative is to let the reader know that I was also a floundering "Aborted Male," unsure, very uncertain, and trying to fake it until I made it at something others would accept as real...and it didn't work for me either. So, I also took this journey and eventually discovered my true potential as a responsible man, as a husband, father, and professional capable of showing up fully and no longer afraid to be present.

CHAPTER FOUR

———◆◆◊◆◆———

NURTURING RESPONSIBILITY— CONFRONTING FEAR, UNCERTAINTY, AND THE EXPECTATIONS TO FAIL

In the journey of the Aborted Male, the nurturing of responsibility becomes a formidable challenge, entangled with the fear of failure, uncertainty, and the weight of societal expectations. Witnessing other men avoid commitments like marriage and fatherhood, he finds himself caught in the grip of a culture that anticipates failure, and he grapples with his own inadequacies and the terror of exposing his vulnerabilities.

The fear of failure looms over him, undermining his confidence and leaving him uncertain about his abilities. It whispers incessant doubts, suggesting that he lacks the knowledge or capability to succeed. The Aborted Male, fearing judgment and rejection, hides his uncertainty, desperate to avoid being exposed as inadequate. This fear becomes a suffocating presence, inhibiting his ability to embrace his responsibilities fully.

To overcome this pervasive fear and the uncertainty that plagues him, the Aborted Male must cultivate self-help skills and adopt a mindset of growth and resilience. Here are some strategies that can assist him in nurturing responsibility:

1. **Embrace Vulnerability:** Recognizing that vulnerability is not a weakness, but a strength, is crucial. By acknowledging and accepting his limitations, the Aborted Male can foster an environment that encourages openness and authenticity. Embracing vulnerability enables him to confront his fears head-on and seek support and guidance when needed.

2. **Challenge Self-Doubt:** The Aborted Male must challenge the self-doubt that hinders his sense of responsibility. By reframing negative self-talk and replacing it with positive affirmations, he can build self-confidence and develop a belief in his own abilities. Engaging in daily affirmations and practicing self-compassion are powerful tools for overcoming the fear of failure.

3. **Seek Knowledge and Support:** Recognizing that nobody knows everything, the Aborted Male must embrace a mindset of continuous learning. Seeking knowledge through self-education, reading books, attending workshops, or engaging in online courses can enhance his skills and understanding. Additionally, seeking support from mentors, coaches, or trusted individuals who have overcome similar challenges can provide guidance and encouragement.

4. **Step Outside the Comfort Zone:** Confronting fear and uncertainty requires the Aborted Male to step outside his comfort zone. By taking calculated risks and engaging in new experiences, he can develop resilience and adaptability. Stepping outside familiar territory allows him to expand his knowledge, confront challenges, and cultivate a sense of responsibility.

5. **Cultivate Self-Reflection:** Regular self-reflection is essential in nurturing responsibility. The Aborted Male should set aside time to assess his strengths, weaknesses, and areas for improvement. Engaging in practices such as journaling, meditation, or therapy can facilitate self-reflection, promote self-awareness, and foster personal growth.

Often the Difference Between Success and Failure Is Sincerity

Often, the difference between success and failure lies in one's ability to practice sincerity. Sincerity is a quality that encompasses honesty, authenticity, and genuine intent. It is the act of aligning our thoughts, words, and actions with our true values and beliefs. When we approach life and our endeavors with sincerity, we create a solid foundation for growth, trust, and meaningful connections.

In the pursuit of success, sincerity becomes a powerful tool. It allows us to build genuine relationships with ourselves and others, fostering trust and collaboration. When we are sincere in our interactions, we establish a reputation for integrity and reliability. People are more likely to gravitate towards those who are sincere, as they provide a sense of authenticity and transparency. Often when we are fearful and uncertain, there is a problem trusting. Often the problem is trusting ourselves to make the right decisions. Sincerity can become an unbiased and protective lens used to confront rationalizations—or in other words, rational lies we create to dissociate or make excuses.

Sincerity also plays a crucial role in personal growth and self-improvement. By practicing sincerity, we are able to confront our strengths and weaknesses with honesty. This self-awareness enables us to make informed decisions, set realistic goals, and work towards continuous self-improvement. Sincere introspection allows us to identify areas for growth and take necessary steps to overcome challenges.

Furthermore, sincerity contributes to effective communication and conflict resolution. When we approach conversations with sincerity, we listen attentively and express ourselves genuinely. This fosters open and honest dialogue, promoting understanding and empathy. By practicing sincerity in our interactions, we can resolve conflicts more effectively, as we genuinely seek resolution rather than perpetuating misunderstandings or harboring hidden agendas.

In the pursuit of success, sincerity goes hand in hand with resilience. When faced with obstacles or setbacks, sincere individuals are more likely to acknowledge their shortcomings and take responsibility for their actions. They learn from their mistakes, adapt their strategies, and persevere with a genuine commitment to their goals. Sincerity allows us to learn from failures and setbacks, transforming them into valuable lessons for growth.

To cultivate sincerity, it is essential to develop self-awareness and reflect on our intentions and motivations. We must strive to align our actions with our values and be true to ourselves and others. Practicing active listening, empathy, and open communication can help foster sincerity in our relationships. It is also crucial to surround ourselves with individuals who value sincerity and encourage our authentic growth.

Sincerity is a powerful attribute that can significantly impact our journey towards success. By practicing sincerity, we build trust, create meaningful connections, and foster personal growth. It is a quality that requires self-reflection, self-improvement, and genuine interactions with others. With sincerity as our guiding principle, we can navigate the challenges of life with integrity, authenticity, and a greater likelihood of achieving our desired success.

Sincerity Is Directional and Not Random

Indeed, sincerity is not a random act but a deliberate and intentional choice. It is a directional approach that involves aligning our thoughts, words, and actions with our true values and intentions. Sincerity requires us to be purposeful in our interactions and to express ourselves genuinely and authentically.

42

When we say that sincerity is directional, we mean that it involves a conscious decision to act in a manner that reflects our true selves. It is about being mindful of our intentions and ensuring that our actions align with our core values. This means that sincerity is not a passive or automatic response but a deliberate effort to be honest, transparent, and true to ourselves and others.

Being sincere in our interactions requires us to consider the impact of our words and actions on others. It involves being aware of how our behavior affects those around us and taking responsibility for the consequences of our choices. Sincerity is about treating others with respect, empathy, and authenticity, even when it may be challenging or uncomfortable to do so.

Directional sincerity also involves self-reflection and self-awareness. It requires us to examine our own motivations, biases, and intentions. By taking the time to understand ourselves better, we can make conscious choices to act in ways that are in alignment with our values and beliefs. This self-reflection helps us to be more sincere in our interactions and to cultivate meaningful connections with others.

Furthermore, sincerity as a directional approach means that it is not a one-time action but an ongoing commitment. It is a continuous practice of self-examination, growth, and improvement. It requires us to constantly evaluate our thoughts, words, and actions and make adjustments as needed to ensure that they are sincere and aligned with our values.

In summary, sincerity is not a random occurrence but a deliberate and intentional choice. It is a directional approach that involves aligning our thoughts, words, and actions with our true values and intentions. By actively choosing sincerity, we can foster genuine connections, build trust, and lead a more authentic and meaningful life.

The Aborted Male Needs to Observe Directional Thinking or Kaizen

Indeed, directional thinking shares similarities with the concept of Kaizen. "Kaizen" is a Japanese term that refers to continuous improvement or change for the better. It emphasizes the idea of making small, incremental changes over time to achieve improvement and growth.

Similarly, directional thinking involves a mindset of continuous improvement and progress. It is about consciously choosing a direction or goal and taking consistent steps towards it. Instead of focusing on sudden and drastic changes, directional thinking encourages small, incremental adjustments that gradually move us closer to our desired outcome.

In the context of sincerity, directional thinking means actively and intentionally striving to improve our ability to be sincere in our thoughts, words, and actions. It requires us to regularly evaluate and reflect on our sincerity and make necessary adjustments to align ourselves more closely with our values and intentions.

Directional thinking in the pursuit of sincerity involves setting clear intentions, defining our values, and consistently practicing behaviors that align with them. It is about making a conscious effort to be more self-aware, empathetic, and authentic in our interactions with others.

Just like Kaizen, directional thinking in sincerity recognizes that change and growth happen over time. It is a gradual process that requires patience, persistence, and a commitment to continuous improvement. By adopting a directional mindset, we can cultivate sincerity as a habit and integrate it into our daily lives.

By applying the principles of Kaizen to directional thinking in sincerity, we can embrace a mindset of ongoing growth and improvement. We can strive to become more sincere individuals by making small, meaningful changes and consistently working towards aligning our thoughts, words, and actions with our true values and intentions.

CHAPTER FIVE

———◆◆◊◆◆———

TRIBAL THINKING AND CO-DEPENDENCY

Tribal thinking refers to a mindset that places a strong emphasis on group identity and loyalty, often at the expense of individual growth and development. Co-dependency, on the other hand, involves relying heavily on others for emotional support and validation, which can hinder personal growth and self-reliance. This is another often used tactic by the modern-day Pharaohs.

Both tribal thinking and co-dependency can indeed pose challenges to the attainment of Kaizen, which promotes individual improvement and self-directed change. When individuals are deeply entrenched in tribal thinking, they may prioritize conformity to group norms and values over personal growth. The pressure to fit in and maintain group harmony can limit their willingness to challenge themselves, explore new ideas, or take risks that are essential for continuous improvement.

Similarly, co-dependency can create a reliance on others for validation and a sense of self-worth. This dependency can hinder personal growth and self-motivated change, as individuals may feel incapable of making decisions or taking actions without the approval or involvement of others. In the context of Kaizen, where individual initiative and self-directed improvement are crucial, co-dependency can impede progress.

To overcome these barriers and foster a state of Kaizen, individuals must cultivate a sense of self-reliance and autonomy. This involves breaking free from tribal thinking by developing an independent identity and mindset that values personal growth and individual expression. It also requires establishing healthy boundaries and reducing dependency on others for validation and decision-making.

Additionally, embracing Kaizen involves cultivating a growth mindset, which entails a belief in one's capacity for learning and improvement. By shifting the focus from external validation to internal motivation and self-reflection, individuals can take ownership of their personal growth journey and pursue continuous improvement independently of external influences.

It is important to note that while tribal thinking and co-dependency can hinder the pursuit of Kaizen, they are not insurmountable obstacles. Through self-awareness, intentional efforts to challenge limiting beliefs and behaviors, and seeking support from individuals who encourage personal growth, individuals can break free from these patterns and embark on their journey of continuous improvement.

Tribal thinking and co-dependency can hinder the achievement of Kaizen by limiting individual growth and self-directed change. However, by cultivating self-reliance, embracing a growth mindset, and seeking supportive relationships, individuals can overcome these barriers and embrace the pursuit of continuous improvement.

References:

1. Brown, B. (2012). *Daring Greatly: How the Courage to Be Vulnerable Transforms the Way We Live, Love, Parent, and Lead*. Avery.

   Neff, K. D. (2011). *Self-Compassion: Stop Beating Yourself Up and Leave Insecurity Behind*. William Morrow Paperbacks.

2. Dweck, C. S. (2007). *Mindset: The New Psychology of Success*. Random House.

3. Covey, S. R. (1989). *The 7 Habits of Highly Effective People*. Free Press.

CHAPTER SIX

CULTIVATING DISCIPLINE AND FOCUS— EMBRACING ZEN AND BUDO PRINCIPLES

In the pursuit of personal growth and transformation, cultivating discipline and focus becomes paramount for the Aborted Male. Drawing inspiration from Zen and Budo philosophies, he can embark on a journey of self-mastery and develop the necessary skills to navigate life's challenges with clarity and resilience. This chapter explores the principles and practices that underpin discipline and focus, guiding the Aborted Male towards a path of self-improvement and inner strength.

A. The Correct Posture Will Produce the Correct Mind

In the realm of Zen and Budo, the importance of correct posture is emphasized as it directly influences one's state of mind. The Aborted Male is encouraged to adopt a physically aligned posture, whether in meditation, martial arts, or daily activities. By aligning the spine, relaxing the muscles, and grounding oneself, he establishes a solid foundation for mental clarity and focus. This correct posture aligns the body's energy and creates a harmonious balance that supports a calm and focused mind.

Practical Exercise: The Aborted Male can practice sitting or standing with an upright posture, paying attention to the alignment of his spine, relaxing the muscles, and feeling a sense of rootedness, stability and breathing. He can integrate this practice into daily activities, such as sitting at his desk or walking, to reinforce the connection between correct posture and a clear state of mind.

B. Get the Nervous System Involved First

In the pursuit of discipline and focus, it is essential to engage the nervous system before attempting any task. This principle, rooted in Zen and Budo, acknowledges the interconnectedness of the mind and body. By activating the nervous system through physical movement or breathwork, the Aborted Male can awaken his senses, heighten his awareness, and prepare his mind for focused action. This intentional engagement of the nervous system sets the stage for increased concentration and mental clarity.

Practical Exercise: The Aborted Male can incorporate mindful movement practices such as yoga, qigong, or martial arts into his routine. By focusing on the breath, synchronizing movement with intention, and being fully present in the physical sensations, he can awaken his nervous system and cultivate a heightened state of awareness. This practice can be integrated as a prelude to important tasks or as a daily ritual to enhance discipline and focus.

C. All Practice Is Education—All Education Is Teaching and Telling

Zen and Budo philosophies emphasize the integration of practice and education. Every action, no matter how seemingly mundane, carries the potential for learning and growth. The Aborted Male is encouraged to approach each practice, whether it be meditation, physical exercise, or daily tasks, with a mindset of curiosity and receptiveness. By adopting an attitude of continuous learning, he can extract valuable insights and lessons from his experiences, thereby deepening his discipline and focus.

Practical Exercise: The Aborted Male can consciously approach his daily activities as opportunities for education and growth. Whether it is washing dishes, walking in nature, or engaging in work-related tasks, he can bring mindfulness to each moment, noticing the sensations, thoughts, and emotions that arise. By observing and reflecting upon these experiences, he can extract valuable lessons and deepen his understanding of himself and the world around him.

Scientific Explanation

The principles derived from Zen and Budo philosophies find support in scientific research. Correct posture has been shown to have a profound impact on cognitive processes, with an aligned and relaxed posture enhancing focus, attention, and overall cognitive performance. Engaging the nervous system through physical movement and breathwork activates the parasympathetic nervous system, promoting relaxation, clarity, and improved cognitive function. This integration of practice and education aligns with the concept of neuroplasticity, which suggests that continuous learning and engagement can lead to the rewiring and strengthening of neural connections, enhancing discipline and focus.

In conclusion, cultivating discipline and focus through the lens of Zen and Budo principles empowers the Aborted Male to navigate life with clarity, resilience, and purpose. By practicing correct posture, engaging the nervous system, and adopting a mindset of continuous learning, he develops the skills necessary for self-mastery and personal growth. These principles, supported by scientific research, offer a transformative path for the Aborted Male to harness his inner strength and embrace a life of discipline and focus.

D. A Caution about Food, Metabolism as One Foundation, and Respecting Constipation for Discipline and Focus

There are certain foods that are scientifically proven to cause anxiety, depression and sluggishness, and lack of focus in thinking. Getting enough sleep and exercise will also improve the life of most people along with a proper diet. Lastly the body is made to move; the circulatory system works for the whole body when there is exercise involved on a regular basis.

So, first and foremost, the impact of nutrition on mental and physical health cannot be underestimated. It is essential to be mindful of the foods we consume, especially those that contain high levels of sugar, as they can interfere with metabolic activity in the body. A diet rich in clean, micronutrient-dense foods that are easy to process is necessary for optimal functioning. By prioritizing whole, unprocessed foods, we can provide our bodies, minds and ability to focus with the necessary nutrients to support cognitive function, mood stability, and overall well-being.

Special Note

The impact of the American diet on men's health is a crucial factor to consider in the restoration process. It is important to acknowledge that certain foods, preservatives, colorings, and additives can interfere with metabolism, particularly at the endocrine level. These foods are known as endocrine disruptors, and they can have negative effects on hormonal balance and overall well-being.

One significant concern is the presence of estrogenic foods in the American diet. Some additives, such as atrazine (found in fertilizers), have been shown to be estrogenic and can interfere with testosterone levels, leading to a reduction in male hormones and masculinity. Processed foods, canned goods, milk, genetically modified organisms (GMOs), and sugars are often consumed without realizing their potential harm. These items can be likened to consuming improvised explosive devices (IEDs), as they can overtax the body and contribute to its breakdown, preventing the Aborted Male from establishing a solid foundation for his health over time.

Furthermore, even drinking water can pose a risk. Some plastic bottles contain bisphenol A (BPA), which can also disrupt endocrine function. These ingredients can interfere with fertility, contribute to erectile dysfunction, and reduce strength and testosterone levels overall. It is alarming to note that many of the food items considered normal in America are actually banned in other countries due to their harmful ingredients.

The normalization of these foods and inadequate attention to nutrition have resulted in detrimental health consequences. The consumption of such items can lead to increased risks of various health conditions, including cancer, metabolic problems, obesity, high blood pressure, diabetes, dementia, heart disease, and fatty liver. These health issues can have a profound impact on overall well-being and quality of life.

To address this issue and restore health, it is crucial for the Aborted Male to reevaluate his dietary choices and prioritize nutrition. Corrective actions should include the following.

1. **Educating oneself:** Learn about the harmful effects of certain foods and additives. Stay informed about nutritional guidelines and research on the impact of the American diet.

2. **Making conscious food choices:** Opt for whole, unprocessed foods whenever possible. Focus on organic fruits and vegetables, lean proteins, and

healthy fats. Limit consumption of processed and sugary foods.

3. **Reading labels:** Develop the habit of reading food labels to identify harmful ingredients. Avoid products that contain high-fructose corn syrup, artificial additives, and preservatives.

4. **Hydration with caution:** Choose drinking water sources that are free from harmful contaminants, such as BPA. Consider using glass or stainless steel containers instead of plastic bottles.

5. **Seeking professional guidance:** Consult with a nutritionist or healthcare provider to create a personalized dietary plan that promotes optimal health and addresses specific concerns.

Furthermore, hydration plays a vital role in maintaining the balance of our bodily functions. Proper hydration ensures that our cells, organs, and systems can operate optimally. Since the human body is composed mostly of water, it is crucial to prioritize drinking enough water throughout the day. Staying well-hydrated promotes healthy metabolism, cognitive clarity, and overall vitality.

Now to constipation, the taboo many generally don't like to talk about. It is another factor that can impede proper metabolism and overall health. By addressing and preventing constipation through dietary fiber intake and adequate hydration, we can support the body's natural detoxification processes and maintain regular bowel movements. This promotes healthy digestion and ensures that our bodies can efficiently eliminate waste and toxins.

Pope John II once stated that Western culture is a culture of death, and this sentiment can be observed in the American diet, which often includes processed foods, excessive sugar, and unhealthy fats. It is crucial to be aware of the impact certain foods can have on our mental and emotional well-being. Some foods like sugar, trans fats, and processed grains can contribute to anxiety, depression, sluggishness, and impaired cognitive function. By being mindful of our food choices and opting for nourishing, whole foods, we can support our mental and emotional health.

Furthermore, ensuring adequate sleep is essential for overall well-being. Sufficient sleep allows our bodies to rest, recover, and rejuvenate. And, during sleep the brain cleans the plaque that builds up during the day as your brain is processing information. Your sleep at night helps clean the brain and this process promotes mental clarity, emotional stability, and optimal cognitive function during the daytime. Prioritizing quality sleep by establishing consistent sleep routines and creating a conducive sleep environment is vital for discipline and focus.

Please keep in mind, the body is designed to move. Regular physical activity is fundamental for maintaining a healthy circulatory system, strengthening muscles, and supporting overall physical and mental health. Engaging in exercise, whether it be through structured workouts, outdoor activities, or simply incorporating more movement into our daily lives, has numerous benefits. It enhances cardiovascular health, promotes the release of endorphins (the body's natural feel-good hormones), and contributes to increased energy levels and improved mood. Keep in mind heart health is mostly electrical capacity. Electricity is generated by the heart muscles, so the cells in the body communicate. To have the trillions of cell processes taking place daily, the heart needs to pump. In summary, the restoration and improvement of human life encompasses not only mental and emotional aspects but also physical well-being. Proper nutrition, hydration, addressing constipation, and adopting a balanced, whole-food diet are crucial for supporting optimal cognitive function and overall health. Adequate sleep and regular physical activity further enhance our well-being, contributing to a fulfilling and vibrant life. By taking care of our bodies and prioritizing these foundational aspects, we can create a solid groundwork for personal growth, discipline, and focus.

So, again constipation is a topic that is often stigmatized, tabooed, and overlooked, yet it can have significant physical and emotional consequences. My personal experience with constipation began in elementary school, when I faced bullying and the fear of using unsupervised public-school bathrooms. This led to me holding in my need to defecate, causing impaction and subsequent visits to the children's hospital. This early encounter with constipation shaped my understanding of its impact on both physical and emotional well-being.

Later in my work as a therapist, I noticed a correlation between constipation and the use of opioids among individuals in my caseload who were struggling with substance abuse. Opioid use is known to increase the frequency of constipation, and many clients reported feeling similar symptoms like that of withdrawal when experiencing constipation. This realization prompted me to delve deeper into the connection between constipation and overall well-being.

In examining constipation and its effects, I found that it goes beyond physical discomfort. Constipation can lead to symptoms such as irritability, abdominal pain, bloating, backaches, lethargy, stress, depression, anxiety, fear, and anger. These physiological and emotional symptoms closely parallel those experienced by my clients during drug withdrawal. The similarities between constipation and withdrawal prompted me to explore the relationship between lifestyle factors, diet, and water consumption.

I discovered that individuals struggling with substance abuse often neglect their water intake, relying instead on sugary beverages. This worsens the conditions for constipation and perpetuates a cycle of discomfort and unhealthy habits. Many resort to using laxatives and suppositories as a quick fix, rather than addressing the root causes through dietary improvements and hydration. Several clients admitted that the discomfort caused by constipation drove them to self-medicate, further exacerbating their substance abuse issues.

Constipation is not merely a matter of physical discomfort; it profoundly affects a person's quality of life. Chronic constipation can be life-threatening, as evidenced by the case of John Wayne, who reportedly had a significant amount of fecal matter in his body at the time of his death.

There have been other instances where severe fecal impaction resulted in medical emergencies and even paralysis.

There was a man in Australia who was so constipated that it caused paralysis in one of his legs. The 53-year-old man came to the emergency room because of the abdominal pain that had building up for three days, and he was suffering from nausea. A rectal examination and a scan of his colon showed he had massive fecal impaction. The impaction was so severe that it was putting pressure on his arteries, cutting off blood flow in some of his organs. Doctors had to surgically remove the fecal matter. This man spent 13 days in the intensive care unit before he was able to walk again. In 2015 it was reported a girl who had a phobia of toilets died because she held her bowel movements until fecal matter started building up in the chest cavity, causing a heart attack. It is really difficult to even think about discipline or focus when you are dealing with constipation for several days or weeks.

It is crucial to recognize the broader context in which constipation occurs. Access to fresh fruits and vegetables are essential for maintaining a healthy diet and is limited in some urban areas designated as "food deserts." This further complicates the issue, making it challenging for individuals in these areas to prioritize their digestive health.

In conclusion, constipation is not just about physical discomfort; it has far-reaching implications for both physical and emotional well-being. The link between constipation and substance abuse highlights the need for comprehensive care that addresses not only the symptoms but also the underlying causes. By promoting education on healthy dietary choices, hydration, and regular bowel movements, we can help individuals break free from the cycle of constipation and improve their overall quality of life. It is essential to destigmatize constipation and openly discuss its impact on mental, emotional, and physical well-being, creating a culture of awareness and support.

CHAPTER SEVEN

——◆◆◇◆◆——

TAKING OWNERSHIP OF FAILURE—
EMBRACING YOUR TRUE POTENTIAL

The statement that "the ruin of a nation starts in the homes of its people" highlights the fundamental role that individuals and families play in shaping the fabric of a society. Similarly, the notion that "the ruin of a person starts with the neglect of his heart" emphasizes the significance of attending to one's emotional and spiritual well-being.

The home, as the foundational unit of society, serves as the primary environment where values, beliefs, and behaviors are nurtured. It is within the family setting that individuals learn essential life skills, develop their character, and form their worldview. When homes are plagued by neglect, dysfunction, or a lack of positive values, the consequences can ripple throughout society, contributing to its decline.

Furthermore, the neglect of one's heart can have profound consequences for personal well-being. The heart, often associated with emotions, desires, and the core of one's being, represents the innermost essence of a person. Neglecting the heart implies disregarding the

61

need for emotional nourishment, self-reflection, and spiritual fulfillment. When individuals fail to nurture their emotional well-being, they may experience a range of detrimental effects, including emotional distress, relationship difficulties, and a diminished sense of purpose.

The consequences of neglecting the heart extend beyond the individual level. When a significant number of people neglect their emotional well-being, it can contribute to a collective sense of disillusionment, apathy, and social fragmentation. The erosion of empathy, compassion, and ethical values in society can further perpetuate cycles of negativity and contribute to the decline of communities and nations.

To address these challenges, it is crucial to prioritize the well-being of individuals and families. Cultivating healthy relationships, promoting emotional intelligence, and fostering a sense of purpose and meaning in life are essential elements in nurturing the heart. This requires dedicating time and effort to self-care, self-reflection, and personal growth. It also entails creating supportive environments that prioritize emotional well-being and provide opportunities for connection, empathy, and personal development.

Additionally, recognizing the interconnectedness between personal and societal well-being underscores the importance of collective responsibility. By promoting positive values, fostering strong communities, and investing in the education and well-being of future generations, societies can create an environment that nurtures the hearts of its people and contributes to the overall flourishing of individuals and nations.

The ruin of a nation starts in the homes of its people, emphasizing the critical role of families and individuals in shaping society. Likewise, the neglect of one's heart can lead to personal decline and have far-reaching consequences. By prioritizing emotional well-being, fostering positive values, and promoting collective responsibility, we can work towards creating a society that values and nurtures the hearts of its people, leading to personal and societal flourishing.

We All have a Noble Birth

Every child of Adam is born of noble birth, with the inherent capacity for success. We enter this world with limitless potential, ready to make our mark in the time we inhabit. However, as we navigate the complexities of life, we encounter negative cultural trends and ideas that can be detrimental to our sense of self-worth and belief in our abilities. These corrosive influences seep into our minds, shaping our thoughts and actions, and planting seeds of doubt and uncertainty.

From an early age, many of us are subjected to societal pressures and expectations that begin to chip away at our self-confidence. Kindergarten becomes a battleground where we are taught to conform, fit in, and measure our worth against external standards. In certain neighborhoods, the challenges are even greater, as the constant exposure to poverty, violence, and limited opportunities can erode our sense of hope and belief in ourselves.

As we grow older, uncertainty and doubt take root, slowly transforming into defining characteristics of our character. We begin to question our abilities, doubting whether we are capable of success in a world that seems stacked against us. The repetitive messages of failure and inadequacy that surround us become internalized, leading us to believe that our destiny is one of perpetual struggle and disappointment.

However, it is essential to recognize that these cultural influences are landmines that we can choose to navigate and overcome. By taking ownership of our failures, we reclaim our power and embrace our true potential. It is a journey of self-discovery and self-empowerment, where we challenge the narratives that have held us back and redefine our own sense of worth.

To take ownership of failure, we must first acknowledge that failure is an inevitable part of the human experience. It is through failures that we learn, grow, and refine our path towards success. Embracing failure as a learning opportunity allows us to release the fear and shame associated with it, freeing ourselves to take risks and pursue our dreams.

In this process, it is crucial to cultivate self-compassion and forgiveness. We must recognize that we are not defined by our failures but by our ability to rise from them. By embracing our imperfections and treating ourselves with kindness and understanding, we create a foundation of self-love that propels us forward.

Another vital aspect of taking ownership of failure is surrounding ourselves with a supportive community. Seeking out mentors, coaches, or like-minded individuals who believe in our potential can provide the encouragement and guidance needed to overcome challenges. Together, we can challenge the negative cultural trends and ideas that have hindered our progress and create a supportive network that fosters growth and resilience.

Additionally, adopting a growth mindset is crucial in taking ownership of failure. Believing that our abilities can be developed through dedication and hard work enables us to see setbacks as temporary roadblocks rather than permanent limitations. This mindset empowers us to persevere, adapt, and continually improve ourselves.

As we navigate the journey of taking ownership of failure, it is vital to remember that success is not solely measured by external achievements or societal standards. It is a deeply personal and individualized pursuit, where each step forward, no matter how small, brings us closer to our true potential.

We all know religion is now almost a curse word in some circles. It has been used for and by every despot and dictator that ever walked the planet. So many have been betrayed by clergy, who used the Bible, Qur'an, and other scriptural texts, but who themselves were pseudo-representatives with a twisted material or domination strategy using G'd. Countries, nations, and humanity have suffered from all types of these social psychopaths, who by using charisma and language, successfully soothed the listener to the point of mass hypnosis, empty their pockets of hard-earned cash or raid the White House in the name of exclusive piety of birth. Those of you who believe in the one G'd, practice your faith; it is the conduit to Nova-level clarity, personal power, and forming a formidable character. However, not only would I also encourage you to pray and pray often, but more importantly live your prayer. To live your prayer would mean that you're involved in your own restoration. In the face of manipulation and the attempts to separate humanity from its true purpose, faith in a higher power can provide certainty, clarity, and righteous purpose. Throughout my 60-plus years of life experience, I have witnessed that those who possess unwavering faith in the Creator of all men/women demonstrate qualities of certainty, boldness, and fearlessness in the face of adversity.

The concept of the Aborted Male explored in this book is just another strategy employed by systems, institutions, and cultural influencers who seek to control and diminish individuals. They aim to make you believe that your failures and struggles are solely your own fault, perpetuating a cycle of self-blame and hopelessness. However, it is crucial to recognize that this narrative is nothing more than a scheme designed to steal your dreams and keep you from reaching your full potential.

For those who believe in the existence of a higher power, **I encourage you to not only pray but also live your** prayer. **It is through living your prayer that you actively engage in your own restoration and transformation.** Your faith serves as a conduit to achieve clarity, personal power, and the development of a formidable character.

However, faith alone is not enough. It must be accompanied by action and a commitment to self-improvement. It is essential to actively participate in your own restoration process, seeking personal growth, and taking responsibility for your actions and choices. This involves embracing discipline, nurturing responsibility, and cultivating a strong sense of self.

By living your prayer and actively engaging in your own restoration, you reclaim your power and reject the false narratives imposed upon you. You become an example of resilience, authenticity, and strength, defying the attempts of manipulators to control and diminish your potential.

In a world filled with manipulation, misinformation, and external influences seeking to shape our thoughts and beliefs, it is vital to hold steadfast to your faith and live your prayer. By doing so, **you become the model you were looking for,** reclaiming your true identity and unleashing your full potential. You can certainly use and observe others to show you, encourage you towards the productive or cultivating path, **but there is nothing more satisfying than recognizing you've become the model or an example of greater excellence yourself."**

Remember, every child of Adam is born of noble birth, destined for greatness, and this is an informed choice. Do not allow the schemes of the manipulators to define your worth or limit your potential. Embrace your faith, cultivate your character, and forge a path of righteousness and authenticity. In doing so, you become a testament to the power of faith and an inspiration to others seeking their own restoration.

In the harsh reality of our world, it is evident that many individuals are deliberately targeted for poverty, pain, and commercial exploitation. The manipulators behind the scenes understand that in order to exert control over the masses, they must weaken the inherent power that every individual is born with. It is a game played out in the shadows, orchestrated by those who seek to maintain their position of power and influence. The appearance and creation of the Aborted Male is not a natural evolution of man. It is a successful experimental scheme that has worked since the Pharaohs of Egypt.

The Power and Conduit of the Subconscious Mind

The power of the subconscious mind is a force that remains largely untapped and underappreciated by the majority of individuals. It exists within each of us, a hidden superpower with the potential to bring about profound transformations in our lives. Unfortunately, its true nature and capabilities are often overlooked or misunderstood, allowing for its exploitation by those who seek to manipulate and control others for their own agendas.

The elite few, educated and knowledgeable about the workings of the subconscious mind, understand its immense power and how to harness it to their advantage.

They recognize that by gaining control over a person's thinking, they can influence their actions and shape their reality. This understanding gives them a significant advantage in molding the minds and beliefs of the general population.

Through various means—such as propaganda, manipulation, and psychological techniques—these individuals exploit the subconscious mind to further their personal agendas. They understand that if they can control what a person thinks, they need not worry about their actions. By determining the thoughts that occupy an individual's mind, they can effectively shape their perception of themselves and the world around them.

One of the ways in which the subconscious mind is manipulated is by making individuals feel inferior. Through a continuous barrage of messages and societal norms, people are made to believe that they are inadequate, unworthy, or flawed in some way. This manipulation leads individuals to seek validation and acceptance from external sources, further reinforcing the control exerted by those in power.

Moreover, if people are made to believe that they are outcasts or social pariahs, they will naturally gravitate towards accepting an inferior status. They may voluntarily segregate themselves or accept mistreatment without being compelled to do so. The subconscious mind, influenced by external forces, drives individuals to conform to the prescribed roles and behaviors dictated by the manipulators.

This exploitation of the subconscious mind occurs on a grand scale, with entire populations falling victim to the schemes of the elite. The consequences are far-reaching, affecting not only individuals' perceptions of themselves but also their relationships, aspirations, and overall quality of life. By keeping people in a state of confusion, doubt, and submission, the manipulators maintain their power and control over the masses.

To break free from the clutches of subconscious manipulation and reclaim personal autonomy, individuals must first recognize the existence and power of their own subconscious mind. This requires education and awareness about the workings of the mind, psychological techniques, and the tactics employed by those seeking to exploit it.

Once armed with this knowledge, individuals can begin the process of reprogramming their subconscious mind, replacing negative and limiting beliefs with empowering and positive ones. Techniques such as visualization, affirmations, meditation, and self-hypnosis can be employed to access and reprogram the subconscious.

By consciously directing their thoughts, individuals can take control of their own minds and shape their reality in alignment with their true desires and values. This process requires commitment, discipline, and a willingness to challenge the dominant narratives and societal norms that have been imposed upon them.

Ultimately, the power of the subconscious mind, when understood and harnessed, becomes a tool for personal transformation and liberation. By tapping into its immense potential, individuals can break free from the chains of manipulation, reclaim their sovereignty, and create a life that is aligned with their authentic selves. It is through this journey of self-discovery and empowerment that one can transcend the limitations imposed by external influences and unlock the true power of the subconscious mind.

For example:

"The conscious and intelligent manipulation of the organized habits and opinions of the masses is an important element in democratic society. Those who manipulate this unseen mechanism of society constitute an invisible government which is the true ruling power of our country ...We are governed, our minds are molded, our tastes formed, our ideas suggested, largely by men we have never heard of. This is a logical result of the way in which our democratic society is organized. Vast numbers of human beings must cooperate in this manner if they are to live together as a smoothly functioning society...In almost every act of our daily lives, whether in the sphere of politics or business, in our social conduct or our ethical thinking, we are dominated by the relatively small number of persons...who understand the mental processes and social patterns of the masses. It is they who pull the wires which control the public mind".

– Edward Bernays, *Propaganda*

There has always been a conscious calculated effort to separate man from his Creator and from Creation

71

Supported Logic. The turmoil in the world is a testament to the success of these strategies. However, certainty, clarity, righteous purpose, boldness, and fearlessness in the face of overwhelming odds are always actively succeeding somewhere. In my life experience, I've witnessed behavior and courage mostly demonstrated by men and women who had faith in the Creator of all men. The Aborted Male, in the context of this book, is just another strategy used by systems, institutions, and cultural influencers who have enough money and resources to hide their filthy hands and make your condition feel like it's entirely your fault; no it's just another type of scheme to steal your dreams.

Trillions of dollars are poured into a vast industry that operates with the sole purpose of ensuring that the masses remain blind and oblivious to the institutional manipulations at play. It is a carefully crafted system designed to distract, mislead, and control. Every effort is made to divert attention and prevent individuals from recognizing their true power and potential, as they are played with like marionettes.

Yet amidst this complex web of manipulation and deceit, there is a glimmer of hope. It is the power of awareness, mindfulness, and caring, of being attentive to the world around us. "When we truly care, nothing goes unnoticed or overlooked." It is through this level of awareness and engagement that we can begin to unravel the intricacies of the system that seeks to suppress our innate power and eventually take the stolen life back.

In the spirit of pure science, we must challenge the status quo and dig deeper to uncover the truth. We must seek out references and online sources that shed light on the hidden agendas and mechanisms of control. It is through this diligent research and exploration that we can arm ourselves with knowledge and insight.

The journey to reclaim our power and break free from the chains of manipulation is not an easy one. It requires resilience, determination, and a willingness to question the narratives that have been imposed upon us. "When you care, nothing gets overlooked." But it is a journey worth embarking on, for within each of us lies the potential to resist, to rise above, and to create a world that aligns with our true values and aspirations.

As we navigate the tumultuous currents of our times, we must remain vigilant and discerning. We must question the information presented to us, recognizing that the truth often lies beyond the surface. By cultivating a critical eye and an unwavering commitment to seeking the truth, we can dismantle the illusions that bind us and forge a path towards freedom and self-empowerment.

In the spirit of Hemingway's concise and direct prose, let us cast aside the veils of deception and delve into the depths of understanding. Through our collective efforts, we can expose the manipulators, reclaim our power, and pave the way for a future characterized by authenticity, justice, and true human potential.

Remember, the power of the subconscious is a force to be reckoned with. It is within our grasp to tap into this wellspring of power and resilience, to defy the odds and transcend the limitations imposed upon us. Let us care deeply, let us seek knowledge, and let us rise above the schemes and manipulations that seek to diminish our worth. Our world has in many places become the domain of one ambush after another. This awareness is not to be paranoid, but to be realistic about what you see, hear, feel, and understand. On every level, seek to understand.

"We now live in a nation where doctors destroy health, lawyers destroy justice, universities destroy knowledge, governments destroy freedom, the press destroys information, religion destroys morals, and our banks destroy the economy".

– Chris Hedges

CHAPTER EIGHT

————◆◆◊◆◆————

OVERCOMING UNCERTAINTY AND BUILDING CONFIDENCE

Uncertainty, a lingering consequence of a deceptive strategy aimed at concealing the power of truth. Agnotology and propaganda, cleverly interwoven with fragments of scientific facts, create the illusion of trust and normalcy. However, beneath the surface lies a web of confusion and dissonance that gradually corrupts the true nature of a growing individual, paving the way for exploitation.

During the formative years, as adolescence gives way to early adulthood, many find themselves in search of an identity. They are bombarded with pseudo-images and icons carefully crafted by myths and media, devoid of any foundation for building a family life, assuming community leadership, or cultivating moral strength rooted in genuine religious beliefs.

But amid this haze of uncertainty, there is a path forward. It requires a shift in mindset and the cultivation of skills to navigate the labyrinth of confusion.

The first step is to recognize the deceptive nature of the forces at play. By understanding that uncertainty is not a natural state, but rather a construct designed to weaken and control, one can begin to dismantle its grip. It is crucial to question the sources of information and scrutinize the narratives presented as truth.

Building confidence in the face of uncertainty demands a commitment to seeking knowledge and embracing lifelong learning. By actively engaging with diverse perspectives, exploring different disciplines, and challenging one's own beliefs, one can develop a broader understanding of the world and gain the confidence to navigate its complexities.

Self-reflection and introspection also play a crucial role in overcoming uncertainty. Taking the time to understand one's values, strengths, and passions provides a solid foundation upon which to build confidence. By embracing authenticity and aligning actions with personal convictions, one can cultivate a sense of purpose and inner strength.

Moreover, developing effective communication skills is vital in navigating the labyrinth of uncertainty. Being able to articulate thoughts, express emotions, and engage in meaningful dialogue not only strengthens personal relationships but also fosters clarity in navigating complex social dynamics. In addition to developing the skills mentioned earlier, it is crucial to address the limiting beliefs and self-doubt that have been ingrained through a lifetime of exposure to deceptive influences, particularly those rooted in tribal thinking. These beliefs can hinder personal growth and prevent individuals from reaching their full potential.

To challenge and overcome these limiting beliefs, it is necessary to engage in a process of self-reflection and introspection. This involves questioning the origins and validity of these beliefs, examining the evidence supporting or refuting them, and consciously choosing to adopt empowering and growth-oriented perspectives.

A key aspect of this process is recognizing that our earlier experiences, especially those influenced by tribal thinking, may have skewed our perception of ourselves and the world around us. Tribal thinking tends to foster an "us versus them" mentality, creating divisions and reinforcing stereotypes that limit our understanding and hinder our ability to connect with others on a deeper level.

To transcend tribal thinking, it is essential to cultivate empathy and open-mindedness. This involves actively seeking out diverse perspectives, engaging in dialogue with individuals from different backgrounds and cultures, and challenging preconceived notions or biases. By broadening our understanding and embracing the richness of human diversity, we can move beyond the limitations imposed by tribal thinking and foster a greater sense of unity and interconnectedness.

Another crucial aspect of challenging limiting beliefs is practicing self-compassion and cultivating a positive self-image. Many individuals who have experienced the effects of tribal thinking may harbor deep-seated feelings of inadequacy or unworthiness. These feelings can manifest as self-doubt, self-criticism, and a persistent fear of not measuring up to societal standards or expectations.

To counteract these negative beliefs, it is important to cultivate self-compassion and develop a positive self-image. This involves acknowledging and accepting one's flaws and imperfections, recognizing that they are an inherent part of being human.

Special Note

Indeed, the mindset can undergo a transformative shift when the mental vocabulary is changed. The internal dialogue plays a crucial role in shaping our perception of ourselves and the world around us. If our thoughts and self-talk mirror the toxic environment we aim to overcome, it becomes difficult to break free from the limitations imposed by that environment.

To initiate change, it is essential to cultivate a new mental vocabulary that is empowering, uplifting, and aligned with our desired growth. This involves consciously choosing words and phrases that inspire confidence, resilience, and a sense of purpose. By replacing negative self-talk with positive affirmations and empowering statements, we can rewire our subconscious mind and create a foundation of self-belief and certainty.

Faith, supported by science, can serve as a powerful conduit for gaining certainty and transforming our mindset. Faith provides a sense of trust and belief in something greater than ourselves, while science offers evidence-based knowledge and understanding of the faith we are trusting. By integrating both faith and scientific principles, we can establish a firm foundation for personal growth and self-improvement.

In addition to developing faith and acquiring knowledge, it is crucial to develop and practice self-regulation skills. Self-regulation involves the ability to manage and control our thoughts, emotions, and behaviors in a constructive and balanced manner. By cultivating self-regulation, we can navigate challenges and setbacks with resilience, maintain focus on our goals, and respond to situations with clarity and composure.

Mobilizing tactical skills is another important aspect of gaining greater confidence. Tactical skills refer to practical strategies and techniques that can be applied in specific situations to achieve desired outcomes. These skills can include effective communication, problem-solving, decision-making, time management, and emotional intelligence. By honing these skills, we can navigate life's challenges with competence and achieve personal and professional success.

It is crucial to recognize that being a man is not about chasing cultural trends or conforming to societal expectations. True manhood lies in bringing culture, in cultivating a sense of purpose, integrity, and contribution. By focusing on personal growth, self-awareness, and living according to one's values, a man can make a positive impact on his own life as well as the lives of those around him.

Changing the mental vocabulary and internal dialogue is a powerful catalyst for transformation. By cultivating a positive and empowering mindset, supported by faith and scientific knowledge, individuals can gain certainty and confidence. Developing self-regulation skills and mobilizing tactical strategies further enhance personal growth and resilience. Embracing the true essence of manhood involves bringing culture and living a purpose-driven life. Through these transformative practices, individuals can break free from the limitations imposed by the modern-day Pharaohs. It is also beneficial to surround oneself with a supportive and empowering community. Connecting with like-minded individuals who share similar goals and values can provide encouragement, accountability, and a sense of belonging. This community can serve as a source of inspiration, guidance, and affirmation as individuals navigate the process of challenging and transforming their limiting beliefs.

However, it is important to acknowledge the journey to overcoming uncertainty is not linear or without obstacles. It requires resilience, patience, and a willingness to confront uncomfortable truths. There may be setbacks and moments of doubt, but by staying true to oneself and persisting in the pursuit of personal growth, one can gradually chip away at the walls of uncertainty and emerge with newfound confidence.

In the spirit of Hemingway's succinct style, let us remember that uncertainty is not an inherent quality, but a construct meant to disempower. By actively challenging the deceptive forces that perpetuate confusion and embracing the skills necessary to navigate uncertainty, we can reclaim our sense of self, forge our own paths, and stand firm in the face of a bewildering world. Remember, as I mentioned earlier, **"you can choose to live well, or die ugly"**.

In the end, it is through the cultivation of self-awareness, lifelong learning, effective communication, and a steadfast commitment to personal growth that we can overcome uncertainty and build the confidence needed to thrive in an ever-changing and complex society.

Some Corrective Actions for Uncertainty

In the realm of uncertainty, where truth is often concealed, a particular strategy emerges. Agnotology and propaganda intertwine, bolstered by fragments of scientific facts that present an illusion of trust and normalcy. Yet beneath this façade lies a web of confusion, carefully crafted to erode the inherent nature of young boys and facilitate exploitation. As they transition into their teenage years and beyond, many young men find themselves in search of an identity, influenced by pseudo-images and icons created by myths and media. However, these false constructs offer no foundation for building a family life, assuming community leadership, or nurturing moral strength rooted in religious principles.

To combat the corrosive effects of uncertainty, corrective actions and skills are crucial. Here are some strategies towards overcoming this challenge:

1. **Critical Thinking:** Encourage young men to question the information presented to them. Teach them to analyze sources, evaluate evidence, and distinguish between fact and opinion. Instilling a habit of critical

thinking helps navigate the maze of misinformation and develops a discerning mind.

2. **Information Literacy:** Equip young men with the skills to access, evaluate, and utilize information effectively. Teach them how to seek reliable sources, fact-check information, and develop a comprehensive understanding of complex issues. By becoming information literate, they can make informed decisions and avoid being swayed by deceptive narratives.

3. **Emotional Intelligence:** Foster emotional intelligence by helping young men develop self-awareness, empathy, and emotional regulation skills. Encourage open communication about feelings, promote empathy towards others, and teach effective coping mechanisms for managing uncertainty and stress.

4. **Authenticity and Self-Reflection:** Encourage young men to explore their values, passions, and beliefs. By fostering self-reflection, they can develop a strong sense of self and authenticity. Emphasize the importance of embracing one's uniqueness and resist the pressures to conform to societal expectations.

5. **Cultivating Resilience:** Teach young men the importance of resilience in the face of uncertainty. Help them develop coping strategies, adaptability, and the ability to bounce back from setbacks.

Emphasize that failures and challenges are opportunities for growth and learning.

6. **Mentorship and Role Models:** Provide young men with positive male role models who embody qualities such as integrity, responsibility, and moral strength. Foster mentorship programs that offer guidance, support, and encouragement to navigate the challenges of uncertainty and build confidence.

7. **Mindfulness and Self-Care:** Promote mindfulness practices that help young men stay grounded in the present moment and manage stress. Encourage self-care activities such as exercise, adequate sleep, and healthy eating habits to support their overall well-being.

8. **Community Engagement**: Encourage young men to actively participate in their communities, fostering a sense of belonging and connection. Engaging in volunteer work or community projects can enhance their confidence, leadership skills, and contribute to positive change.

9. **Education and Lifelong Learning:** Instill a love for learning and a curiosity to explore various subjects. Encourage continuous education, whether through formal schooling or self-directed learning. Emphasize the value of knowledge and the power it brings to navigate uncertainty.

10. **Faith and Spirituality:** For those who seek it, guide young men towards exploring faith and spirituality as sources of strength and guidance. Encourage

them to connect with their beliefs, engage in meaningful rituals, and seek support from religious communities.

Through the implementation of these few corrective actions, young men can navigate the fog of uncertainty, unravel the illusions presented by agnotology and propaganda, and cultivate the confidence needed to forge their own paths. By equipping them with critical thinking skills, emotional intelligence, authenticity, resilience, positive role models, and a sense of purpose, we empower them to overcome uncertainty and build a foundation of strength, integrity, and moral character.

CHAPTER NINE

———◆◆◇◆◆———

MATERIALISM, THE "GAME," AND CULTIVATING NEW VALUES

The world of the Aborted Male is one marred by the allure of materialism and the delusions of social image. From a young age, he may have experienced various traumas and setbacks that hindered his progress and development. If his upbringing was marked by drugs, violence, gambling, and a constant partying atmosphere, it would have distorted his understanding of what is considered "normal." The neglect and criminal mindset prevalent in his environment deprived him of the necessary milestones and guiding influences that could have shaped his purpose and direction in life.

Without the proper guidance and nurturing, the aborted male is left to navigate the world with a stunted imagination, mistakenly believing he is forging a unique path when, in reality, he is merely following in the footsteps of ancestral misguided tribal influencers. Interference in certain communities perpetuates dysfunction, perpetuating a cultural trance orchestrated by those unseen powers in control. This young man, devoid of real examples to guide him towards cultivating, building, and correcting, is left with limited options. Crime, co-dependence, and conformity to aimless peer groups become his default choices, aligning his character with the distorted mindset prevalent in his environment.

Manufactured and scripted, his mind is confined to the confines of mindless entertainment, where he spends hours engrossed in video games that offer temporary escape but little substance. He becomes a devoted fan of anything that promises group acceptance, even going so far as to brand himself like cattle in a misguided attempt to embody some primitive notion of manhood. His discussions revolve around the game, but he fails to grasp the true nature of the game itself.

The game, in many cases, involves transactions between individuals who are both aware of the potential for lies and deception. Both parties accept the possibility of fraud, understanding that it may be a "get over." Whether drugs or illicit goods are involved, the buyer knows there is a risk, just as the seller knows the money received could be counterfeit. In these communities, the Aborted Male accepts criminality as the norm, as it appears that everyone around him is also involved in similar activities.

To address the challenges faced by the Aborted Male and guide him towards a different path, corrective measures must be implemented. Here are some key strategies:

1. **Education and Awareness**: Provide comprehensive education that exposes the realities of criminal behavior and its consequences. Highlight the long-

term negative impact on individuals, families, and communities affected by crime.

2. **Mentorship and Role Models:** Offer positive male role models who demonstrate integrity, responsibility, and moral strength. Mentorship programs can provide guidance, support, and inspiration for young men seeking a path of purpose and growth.

3. **Community Support:** Foster a supportive community environment that encourages personal development, resilience, and the pursuit of meaningful goals. Engage community members in initiatives that promote positive values and discourage criminal behavior.

4. **Access to Resources:** Ensure that individuals in marginalized communities have access to resources and opportunities that promote personal and professional growth. This includes access to education, job training, mental health services, and recreational activities.

5. **Empowerment and Self-Esteem:** Instill a sense of empowerment and self-worth in young men through programs that build self-esteem, develop leadership skills, and encourage personal growth.

6. **Addressing Trauma:** Provide trauma-informed care and therapeutic interventions for individuals who have experienced trauma. This includes offering counseling services, support groups, and trauma-

focused therapies to help address underlying issues and promote healing.

7. **Encouraging Critical Thinking**: Foster critical thinking skills that enable young men to question societal norms, challenge harmful influences, and make informed decisions. Teach them to analyze information critically, separate fact from fiction, and seek evidence-based knowledge.

8. **Promoting Cultural Identity:** Emphasize the importance of cultural pride and heritage, allowing young men to connect with their roots and develop a positive sense of identity. This can help counteract the negative influences of a distorted environment.

9. **Family Support and Involvement:** Engage families in the process by providing support, resources, and guidance to parents and caregivers. Strengthening family bonds and promoting healthy relationships can contribute to the overall well-being and positive development of young men.

10. **Addressing Societal Inequities:** Tackle the root causes of societal inequities that perpetuate crime and dysfunction in certain communities. Advocate for social justice, equal opportunities, and systemic changes that address poverty, discrimination, and lack of access to resources.

By implementing these corrective measures, we can begin to uplift the aborted male from the cycle of crime, violence, and exploitation. Through education, mentorship, community support, and a focus on personal growth, we can guide young men towards a path of purpose, resilience, and moral strength. It is through these collective efforts that we can break the chains that hold them captive and empower them to redefine their lives and build a better future.

CHAPTER TEN

———◆◆◇◆◆———

CULTIVATING HEALTHY RELATIONSHIP

The journey of the Aborted Male towards personal growth and fulfillment extends to his ability to foster healthy relationships. The past experiences and distorted influences he has encountered may have hindered his understanding of what it means to establish meaningful connections with others. However, through the development of self-regulation skills, emotional intelligence, mindfulness practices, and diplomatic approaches inspired by Zen teachings, the aborted male can improve his ability to cultivate healthy relationships. The following steps provide a roadmap for him to embark upon this transformative journey:

1. **Self-Regulation Skills: a. Identify triggers.** Develop self-awareness to recognize personal triggers that lead to reactive behavior in relationships. **b. Pause and reflect.** Practice taking a moment to pause, breathe, and reflect before responding impulsively to situations or conflicts. **c. Emotional regulation.** Learn techniques to manage and express emotions effectively, such as deep breathing, journaling, or seeking professional support.

2. **Emotional Intelligence: a. Self-awareness.** Enhance understanding of personal emotions, strengths, weaknesses, and values. **b. Empathy.** Cultivate the ability to understand and share the feelings of others, developing compassion and active listening skills. **c. Emotional management.** Learn to recognize and regulate emotions in oneself and others, fostering healthier communication and conflict resolution.

3. **Mindfulness Practices: a. Daily mindfulness meditation.** Dedicate a few minutes each day to engage in mindfulness meditation, focusing on the present moment and cultivating a non-judgmental awareness of thoughts and emotions. **b. Mindful communication.** Practice active listening, being fully present and attentive during conversations, and responding with intention and clarity. **c. Gratitude practice.** Cultivate gratitude for the people in one's life, acknowledging their positive qualities and expressing appreciation.

4. **Diplomacy in a Zen Way: a. Seek understanding.** Approach conflicts with a genuine desire to understand the other person's perspective, fostering open and non-judgmental dialogue. **b. Non-attachment.** Practice letting go of personal expectations and attachments to outcomes, allowing for greater flexibility and acceptance in relationships. **c. Non-violent communication.** Adopt compassionate and non-aggressive communication techniques, focusing on expressing needs and

feelings assertively while respecting the dignity of others.

Challenging Profanity, an Aborted Male Identifier

The Aborted Male faces significant challenges in establishing healthy communication patterns due to his blunt and often profane vocabulary, closed mindset resulting from street experiences, and limited understanding of emotional intelligence. Furthermore, the tendency for many to become intoxicated to dissociate from the painful pseudo-male experiences further hampers his use of executive functioning abilities, betraying the false image he tries to portray as a man. His clouded mental state is evident in his banter, and his toxic lifestyle and values make others cautious and wary of his presence and inflated ego. He is often quick to argue without understanding, resorting to violence as an ego response to protect his damaged social image, or curse you out with his penitentiary vocabulary. However, there are corrective measures and a wealth of knowledge, skills, and resources available to guide the Aborted Male toward a path of growth and improved communication. The following corrections and references can help him navigate this transformative journey:

1. **Expanding Vocabulary and Communication Style: a. Correction:** Replace blunt and profane language with a more respectful and constructive vocabulary. **b. Reference:** *Words That Work: It's Not What You Say, It's What People Hear,* by Frank Luntz.

2. **Open-Mindedness and Growth Mindset: a. Correction:** Encourage an open mindset that embraces new ideas, perspectives, and experiences. **b. Reference:** *Mindset: The New Psychology of Success*, by Carol S. Dweck.

3. **Emotional Intelligence: a. Correction:** Develop emotional awareness and regulation skills to better understand and express emotions. **b. Reference:** *Emotional Intelligence: Why It Can Matter More Than IQ*, by Daniel Goleman.

4. **Substance Abuse and Executive Functioning: a. Correction:** Address substance abuse issues to improve executive functioning abilities and decision-making skills. **b. Reference:** *Rewired: A Bold New Approach to Addiction and Recovery*, by Erica Spiegelman.

5. **Active Listening and Empathy: a. Correction:** Cultivate active listening skills to truly understand others and respond empathetically. **b. Reference:** *Nonviolent Communication: A Language of Life*, by Marshall B. Rosenberg.

6. **Conflict Resolution and Anger Management: a. Correction:** Learn effective strategies for resolving conflicts without resorting to violence and managing anger in a healthy manner. **b. Reference:** *The Dance of Anger: A Woman's Guide to Changing the Patterns of Intimate Relationships*, by Harriet Lerner.

7. **Continuous Learning and Personal Development: a. Correction:** Embrace a lifelong learning mindset to

expand knowledge, broaden perspectives, and improve communication skills. **b. Reference:** *The 7 Habits of Highly Effective People: Powerful Lessons in Personal Change*, by Stephen R. Covey

CHAPTER ELEVEN

---◆◆◇◆◆---

CONFINING SELF-HATE AND CULTIVATING SELF-LOVE

The Aborted Male, in his struggle to imitate real manhood, lives each day in fear of being discovered, burdened by the weight of his hidden emotions. He exists in a constant state of discomfort, never truly at ease, always uncertain about when his façade will crumble. Finding solace in the company of others who share his self-hate, he hides and blends in, hoping to evade the spotlight that would expose his insecurities. Self-confidence eludes him, leaving him dependent on the collective rather than standing as an individual. The path he chooses is one of dissociation, seeking temporary relief in the pursuit of fleeting dopamine rushes. He becomes well-versed in the latest distractions, using them as a means to escape from the responsibilities of a responsible man who cultivates, produces, builds, and accepts self-management, self-regulation, and leadership.

Lacking self-love, the Aborted Male denies himself kindness and fails to recognize the uniqueness of his own human capital. Instead, he willingly conforms to the stereotypes that characterize this dysfunctional group he has become a part of. Unaware of the forces that shaped him, he remains trapped in a dysfunctional mindset, conditioned to perceive language and life through distorted lenses.

Yet deep within him lies the potential for change and transformation. The journey toward confining self-hate and cultivating self-love requires a shift in perception and a reevaluation of his worth. It is a process of breaking free from the chains of self-denigration and embracing the power of self-acceptance. By recognizing his inherent value and acknowledging his own unique qualities, the Aborted Male can begin to build a foundation of self-love.

This transformation requires:

1. **Self-Reflection and Awareness:** The aborted male must engage in deep self-reflection to understand the origins of his self-hate and the impact it has on his life. By becoming aware of his own thought patterns and behaviors, he can begin the process of unraveling the conditioning that led to his current state.

2. **Challenging Negative Beliefs:** He must actively challenge the negative beliefs and self-limiting narratives that perpetuate self-hate. This involves questioning the validity of these beliefs and replacing them with more empowering and compassionate perspectives.

3. **Cultivating Self-Compassion:** The Aborted Male must learn to extend kindness, forgiveness, and understanding to himself. By treating himself with the same compassion he would offer to others, he

can begin to heal the wounds of self-hate and embrace a more loving relationship with himself.

4. **Embracing Personal Growth:** He must commit to personal growth and development, seeking opportunities for learning, self-improvement, and self-discovery. This can involve pursuing education, engaging in meaningful hobbies, and setting goals that align with his authentic desires.

5. **Surrounding Himself with Positive Influences:** The Aborted Male should seek out individuals who uplift and support his journey toward self-love. Surrounding himself with positive influences, such as mentors, role models, and supportive friends, can help reshape his perspective and foster a healthier self-image.

6. **Seeking Professional Help:** In some cases, seeking the guidance of a therapist or counselor can be beneficial. A trained professional can provide tools and techniques to navigate the complexities of self-hate, facilitating the healing process and promoting self-love.

It is through these steps and a commitment to ongoing self-work that the Aborted Male can confine self-hate and nurture self-love. While the journey may be challenging, the rewards of self-acceptance, inner peace, and a genuine sense of fulfillment are within reach. By recognizing his own worth and embracing the beauty of his unique existence, he can transcend the limitations imposed upon him, reclaim his power, and build a life guided by self-love and authenticity.

CHAPTER TWELVE

---◆◆◊◆◆---

EMBRACING AUTHENTIC MANHOOD AND PERSONAL GROWTH

Throughout this book, we have embarked on a journey to unravel the complexities of the Aborted male, examining the societal factors, personal struggles, and internalized beliefs that contribute to his sense of disconnection and self-doubt. We have explored various aspects of personal growth, ranging from self-awareness and emotional intelligence to mindfulness, physical well-being, and spiritual alignment. Now it is time to bring together the knowledge and skills acquired in each chapter and ignite a call to action for those men who find themselves trapped in the confines of the stereotypical Aborted Male.

Physical Growth: Taking Care of the Temple

We have emphasized the importance of physical well-being as a foundational element in reclaiming one's manhood. Engaging in regular exercise, adopting a holistic diet, and prioritizing proper hydration are essential steps towards nurturing the body. Additionally, understanding the impact of substances and addictive behaviors can empower men to make conscious choices that align with their desired self-image.

Emotional Growth: From Self-Hate to Self-Love

The journey towards emotional growth begins with self-reflection, cultivating self-compassion, and challenging negative beliefs. By embracing vulnerability, developing emotional intelligence, and learning effective self-regulation skills, men can create space for authentic connections and healthy relationships. It is through understanding and managing their emotions that they can truly experience personal growth and fulfillment.

Spiritual Growth: Connecting to the Divine Within

Spiritual growth involves exploring one's beliefs, connecting with a higher power, and developing a sense of purpose. By recognizing the power of faith and engaging in practices such as prayer, meditation, and mindfulness, men can cultivate inner peace, find guidance in times of uncertainty, and align their actions with their values. Spiritual growth allows men to tap into their inner strength and find meaning in their journey.

Intellectual Growth: Expanding the Mind—Developing the Third Eye

"When you care, nothing gets overlooked" is a powerful mindset that can be likened to the concept of the third eye. The third eye, often associated with intuition and inner vision, represents an elevated state of consciousness and heightened awareness.

Caring deeply about something or someone requires a genuine investment of attention, empathy, and concern.

It goes beyond surface-level engagement and involves a deeper connection and understanding. When you truly care, you are attuned to the nuances, details, and subtleties that might otherwise go unnoticed.

In this sense, caring acts as a metaphorical third eye that enables you to perceive beyond what is immediately visible. It allows you to see beneath the surface, delve into the underlying emotions and motivations, and gain insight into the intricacies of a situation or person.

Having this mindset of caring and attentiveness opens up a world of possibilities. It helps you cultivate empathy, as you actively seek to understand others and their experiences. It also promotes mindfulness, as you strive to be fully present and engaged in each moment.

With the third eye of caring, you become more attuned to the needs of others, as well as your own. You become aware of the small details that can make a significant difference, and you prioritize giving attention to the things that truly matter.

Moreover, the third eye of caring empowers you to extend compassion and support to others. It allows you to offer a listening ear, a helping hand, or a comforting presence. By paying attention to the needs and concerns of those around you, you contribute to creating a more compassionate and interconnected world.

Importantly, the third eye of caring also encompasses self-care and self-awareness. It reminds you to extend the same level of attention and compassion to yourself, acknowledging your own needs, feelings, and well-being.

In conclusion, when you care deeply, you activate the metaphorical third eye that heightens your awareness and perception. This mindset allows you to see beyond the surface, understand others and yourself more profoundly, and create meaningful connections. By cultivating this caring mindset, you enrich your own life and positively impact the lives of those around you.

A Call to Action: Embrace Your Authenticity

To the men who resonate with the struggles of the Aborted Male, it is time to take action and reclaim your authentic manhood. The journey towards transformation requires courage, perseverance, and a willingness to step outside of your comfort zone. Recognize that you are not alone in this pursuit, as countless men have walked a similar path and found liberation.

Begin by embracing self-acceptance and love. Challenge the false narratives that have been ingrained within you and redefine your self-worth. Surround yourself with positive influences, seek support from like-minded individuals, and find mentors who can guide you on your journey. Engage in self-reflection, exploring the depths of your emotions and beliefs, and be willing to face the discomfort that comes with growth.

Commit to a holistic approach to personal development. Nurture your physical well-being through regular exercise, a balanced diet, and proper self-care. Cultivate emotional intelligence, develop self-regulation skills, and forge genuine connections with others. Connect with your spirituality, finding solace and purpose in your beliefs. Expand your intellectual horizons, embracing a thirst for knowledge and critical thinking.

Remember, this is a lifelong journey, and growth takes time. Be patient and kind to yourself, celebrating each step forward and learning from setbacks. Surround yourself with a community of support, seeking guidance from professionals when needed. You have the power to break free from the confines of the Aborted Male and emerge as a man who is authentic, resilient, and capable of making a positive impact on the world.

Right now, it is time to reject the limitations imposed by society and reclaim your true essence. Embrace the skills and knowledge acquired throughout this book as tools for personal growth and transformation. You have the power to rewrite your narrative, transcending the stereotypes and cultural influences that have held you back. Embrace your authenticity, ignite your spirit, and embark on a journey of self-discovery and fulfillment. The world is waiting for the emergence of the man you were meant to be. Seize this moment and let your light shine brightly.

CHAPTER THIRTEEN

------◆◆◇◆◆------

THE BRIGHT MOMENTS AND THE GRIEVING

Transforming oneself from an Aborted Male to a responsible male creates both bright moments and grieving. Grieving will come because the friends who you associated with but remain involved in dysfunctional and dissociative activities will no longer be in alignment with your new path in life. During this time, it's very important for you to consciously be comfortable because it is a choice, while you are experiencing being uncomfortable listening to a polluted subconscious that has not yet changed. Eventually, you will meet someone that you've never met before and that is when the bright moments take place. To finally be present with yourself, without shame, without disappointment, or regrets and finally satisfied with your mirror image is so satisfying. For most, make the journey of being kind to themselves for the first time and having no real regrets for the first time and practicing self-love and kindness is truly a step towards recovering the original innocent nature and it all feels like the first time. Because the tactics and strategies used to produce the Aborted Male by the modern-day Pharaoh started often in early childhood. So yes, for many who are fortunate to recover from this dysfunctional way of living, it feels like the first time they've truly met someone they like. Your previous friends, and others, will notice the change before you even meet this person, and because of this growing strength, envy and jealousy may follow. So don't expect to fit in, because you won't. Don't expect to be immediately accepted by your friends; maybe you will, but most likely you won't. Live your life, don't brag, don't get showy, remain grateful, and continue to evolve. Now your responsibility is your journey on a new path bringing in a new culture, one that you've created and excepted as a conduit for change, with the help of G'd, science, new understanding, new thinking, and purposeful intentional directed behavior.

Epilogue: The Transformative Lifelong Practice

The restoration process of the Aborted Male begins with the realization that not fitting in is actually freedom. It is a freedom that can be accessed by embracing transformation through the word of God. Scripture provides guidance and wisdom that, when coupled with scientific observations, opens up new levels of understanding of the unseen aspects of life.

Step 1: Translating Scripture and Scientific Observations. Start by delving into Scripture and identifying verses or teachings that resonate with your journey of restoration. Look for connections between these teachings and scientific observations. Seek to understand how the principles and insights from both sources can complement and enhance each other. This process of translation allows you to bridge the gap between faith and empirical knowledge.

Step 2: Incorporating New Information. Once you have identified the relevant insights from Scripture and scientific observations, it's time to incorporate them into your life. Take these new understandings and apply them as behavioral practices. Begin to integrate them into your daily routines and interactions, actively seeking ways to embody the wisdom they offer. Be open to learning and adapting as you explore this new territory.

Step 3: Building Discipline and Habit. As you engage in these new practices, focus on building discipline around them. Consistency is key. Make a conscious effort to repeat these practices regularly until they become habits. By consistently implementing the behavioral changes that align with your newfound insights, you strengthen their impact on your life.

Step 4: Gaining Confidence and Competence. With consistent practice, you will begin to notice positive changes and improvements in various areas of your life. These changes will contribute to a growing sense of confidence and competence. Recognize and celebrate your progress, and let it fuel your motivation to continue on this path of restoration.

Step 5: Working Towards Mastery. While competence is an important milestone, aim for mastery. As you gain proficiency in living out the principles and wisdom acquired through Scripture and scientific observations, strive to refine and deepen your understanding. Seek opportunities for further growth and development, embracing a mindset of continuous improvement.

Step 6: Turning Wisdom into Lifestyle. As you internalize the principles and insights, let them shape your lifestyle. Allow them to permeate every aspect of your being, influencing your thoughts, choices, and actions. Make conscious decisions that align with the wisdom you have gained, cultivating a way of living that reflects your restored self.

Step 7: Sharing Wisdom and Impacting Others. The wisdom you have acquired through this restoration process is not meant to be hoarded but shared with others. As you embody the transformed version of yourself, be an example to those around you. Share your experiences, insights, and practices with others, helping them on their own journey of restoration and personal growth.

Through these steps, you can gradually move towards life mastery or greater personal certainty. It is a journey of continuous learning, growth, and transformation. Embrace the process, remain open to new discoveries, and let the wisdom gained guide you in your pursuit of a restored and purposeful life.

This tactical workbook and lifestyle guide serves as a condensed and focused narrative that addresses the causes, problems, characteristics, and solutions to support the growth and development of males into men who are loved and respected by women and the rest of the world. It is specifically designed to dismantle and undo the schemes implemented by the modern-day Pharaohs who seek to diminish and weaken the potential of men.

By diving into the core issues and challenges faced by males in our society, this guide provides valuable insights and strategies to overcome these obstacles and reclaim one's true identity as a strong and honorable man. It sheds light on the influences and tactics employed by those who seek to manipulate and control; and empowers individuals to rise above these schemes.

Through a combination of self-reflection, knowledge acquisition, practical exercises, and actionable steps, this guide offers a comprehensive approach to personal growth and transformation. It encourages individuals to challenge their limiting beliefs, reshape their mindset, and cultivate the qualities and behaviors that exemplify true manhood.

The focus is on unraveling the web of deception and reclaiming one's authentic self. It guides individuals through the process of self-discovery, self-awareness, and self-improvement. By providing practical tools and techniques, it enables individuals to develop resilience, emotional intelligence, communication skills, and leadership qualities that garner love, respect, and admiration.

This guide recognizes the importance of dismantling the influence of the modern-day Pharaohs, who seek to diminish and control the potential of men. It empowers individuals to break free from the societal norms and expectations imposed upon them, and instead embrace their own unique path towards personal greatness.

Ultimately, this tactical workbook and lifestyle guide serves as a powerful resource to guide individuals on their journey towards becoming the men they are destined to be. It offers a roadmap to undo the schemes and manipulations of the modern-day Pharaohs, and instead, cultivates a new paradigm of strength, integrity, and purpose. By following the guidance and implementing the strategies outlined within, individuals can reclaim their true identity, earn the love and respect they deserve, and make a positive impact in their own lives and the world around them. Please keep in mind, to create any healing space, be kind to yourself.